Zion Still Sings

For Every Generation

Pew Edition

Abingdon Press
Nashville, Tennessee

ZION STILL SINGS
Pew Edition

This book is printed on recycled, acid-free paper.

ISBN 978-0-687-33527-5

07 08 09 10 11 12 13 14 15 16 — 10 9 8 7 6 5 4 3 2 1

MANUFACTURED IN THE UNITED STATES OF AMERICA

Contents

Foreword

More than twenty-five years ago, in 1981, *Songs of Zion* was published and became a favorite of people and congregations in many denominations across the nation and around the world. Like previous collections of Christian music, it included treasured melodies and texts of deep and hallowed memory. The songs brought to mind days gone by and people who touched and shaped lives. It also contained expressions of the faith wrapped in fresh renderings sung by a new generation of Christians. The songs sprang largely from the Black religious experience, and the life and legacy of African Americans. Nevertheless, the message of pain, suffering, hope, and salvation resonated with people of many racial and ethnic backgrounds, who embraced the selections in *Songs of Zion* and found meaning and inspiration in them. In the end, songs belong uniquely to those who sing them.

Every generation sings its song of Zion, praising God in the sanctuary. And for twenty-five years, new songs have been pouring forth. Each new generation creates songs borne out of its experiences and circumstances, not merely those of former generations and eras. Exciting new genres of music have emerged with their own message of joy, pain, suffering, challenge, and hope. Hence the need for a compilation that captures the songs and rhythms of the future/present even while linking them to more traditional songs that have stood the test of time—a resource entitled *Zion Still Sings: For Every Generation*.

For nearly three years, a generationally diverse group representing talented and gifted church musicians, clergy, composers, and theological school faculty members from across the church has worked together to produce a new collection of the songs of faith that captures the best musical practice and tradition in African American churches today. *Zion Still Sings* will encompass music that is new and different, as well as the old and familiar. The committee also commissioned the composition of new texts and new tunes.

With *Zion Still Sings,* we believe we have created another valuable resource for the church and for all Christians who are compelled to sing the songs of Zion. This new book is not intended to replace *Songs of Zion* or any of the rich variety of worship resources already available to help people sing their faith with enthusiasm. Instead, it offers a resource that contains songs that will aid the spiritual formation of the Body of Christ, that old ship of Zion, as we are firmly established in the twenty-first century.

It is our hope that congregations will learn to love and value *Zion Still Sings*. Perhaps there are those who have been looking for new melodies and rhythms and will find them here, thus being able to sing the songs of faith as never before. There may even be those who have never before sung the songs of a faith rooted in Jesus Christ. Perhaps they will hear these songs and be touched and inspired by the music and message, so much so that they will choose to be numbered among the singing faithful.

In a world of continued strife, brokenness, despair, and hopelessness, we trust that this new songbook will be further evidence that even in such a world—for every generation—*Zion Still Sings!*

Bishop Woodie W. White, Retired
Chairperson

Preface

The work of this project began during the 2000–2004 quadrennial with the positing of such an idea to Neil Alexander, President and Publisher of The United Methodist Publishing House. Following the widespread acceptance across ecumenical lines and the continuing sales of *Songs of Zion* more than twenty years after its first printing, the project to contemporize and expand musical offerings in a new songbook was met with a great degree of interest and support.

The gathering of this collection of songs and music of *Zion Still Sings: For Every Generation* has been a labor of love and an act of worship for the Editorial Committee. During the last two years, the Committee members considered trends in African American worship, heard from numerous others through their participation in surveys, relied on our personal instincts and experiences, and benefited from the insights and wisdom of an ecumenical group of expert consultants, as we poured over hundreds of wonderful songs seeking to honor our purpose statement for this collection.

In the spirit of honoring and preserving the richness and inclusiveness of our African American musical heritage in worship:

1. *This resource will celebrate the diversity of styles, genres, and performance practices that are rendered in praise to God.*
2. *This resource will offer up new music that will inspire and challenge persons to see God with new eyes.*
3. *This resource will seek to motivate those outside the church to come to know God.*
4. *This resource will not compromise the theological and biblical integrity of the church.*
5. *This resource, in the spirit of Matthew 28:19, will serve as a motivating force for persons to "do" the gospel.*

I acknowledge with grateful appreciation the pioneering efforts of those who gave us *Songs of Zion* and the members of the Editorial Committee of *Zion Still Sings: For Every Generation* who are determined to keep Zion singing.

Bishop Woodie W. White, Chair	Dean B. McIntyre
*William B. McClain, Chair of Texts	Mark A. Miller
*Cynthia Wilson, Chair of Tunes	Marilyn E. Thornton, Music Editor
Gennifer Brooks	Charlene Ugwu, Project Manager
Cecilia L. Clemons	Bob MacKendree, Music Resources, UMPH
Marlon Hall	Bill Gnegy, Music Resources, UMPH
Monya Davis Logan	Gary Smith, Music Resources, UMPH
Henry Masters, Sr.	

Finally, we are grateful to all who have helped in any way.

Myron F. McCoy
General Editor

*Members of *Songs of Zion* Editorial Committee

Just a Few Words

God meets us in every situation, for every generation, and in every location. That's what we mean by *Zion Still Sings*. Zion is where we meet God. When heads were bowed down with the oppression of slavery, a song would come forth such as "Guide My Feet" or "I Want Jesus to Walk with Me" and God would be there, lifting heads and hearts. God was in the hush arbors, the segregated galleries, the mission churches, and in the churches built from used bricks, as the community sang hymns such as "At the Cross" and "Yield Not to Temptation," gaining the assurance that God's kingdom was inclusive.

God was present in Historically Black Colleges and Universities where many who contributed to this collection received training and teach: Howard University (Washington, DC), Bluefield State (WV), Dillard (LA), Bethune-Cookman College (FL), Interdenominational Theological Center (GA), and Tennessee State University. God was present when doors began to open, giving opportunities to learn and teach at places like Juilliard (NY), Peabody Conservatory (MD), Drew University (NJ), Eastman School of Music (NY), Vanderbilt Divinity School (TN), and many other fine state and private institutions.

Zion Still Sings because just as God was present during the Great Migration with Charles Tindley and Kenneth Morris, just as God was present during the Civil Rights Movement when we sang "Ain't Gonna Let Nobody Turn Me 'Round," God meets the current generation in the streets of our 21st-century world. God will meet you with "It's Incredible," using call and response in a way that the ancestors would never have dreamed. God will be present as you rap out "Heavenly Father" and interpret the prayer of Jesus for post-moderns. God will meet you in the contemporary jazz tones of a song for ushers, "Step," and the upbeat, 12-bar blues of "All Around Me!" a song that echoes the biblical truth that God is so high, so low, and so wide. God is inclusive.

There were many contributors to *Zion Still Sings* with submissions from every location, situation, and generation—truly a community effort. The songbook has two editions, Pew and Accompaniment. The Pew Edition has all vocals needed for congregational participation with specific instructions concerning songs that may be linked in medleys. The Accompaniment Edition includes piano accompaniment, synthesizer, and percussion parts. Some songs are exactly the same in both editions, usually four-part hymn style. Thanks and acknowledgments to the Music Resources Unit at Abingdon Press and to a community of gifted and competent musicians, who composed, transcribed, arranged, edited, and typeset music. The production team included:

William S. Moon	Julianne Eriksen
Allen Tuten	Gary Alan Smith
Charlene Ugwu (Project Manager)	Bob MacKendree
Bill Gnegy	Debi Tyree

May you enjoy the fruit of this labor of love, *Zion Still Sings: For Every Generation.*

Marilyn E. Thornton,
Music Editor for *Zion Still Sings*

All Around Me!   1

Where can I go from your spirit? Or where can I flee from your presence? If I ascend to heaven, you are
there; if I make my bed in Sheol, you are there. If I take the wings of the morning and settle at the farthest
limits of the sea, even there your hand shall lead me, and your right hand shall hold me fast.
(Psalm 139:7-10)

1. God is high,   God is low,   God is wide   and he
2. God is here,   God is there,   God is great   and he's
3. God is in,   God is out,   God's so good   that it

loves me so,   all a-round me,   oh yes,   all a -
ev - ery-where   all a-round me,   oh yes,   all a -
makes me shout   all a-round me,   oh yes,   all a -

round me.   So   high, so   low,   so
round me.   So   here, so   there, so
round me.   So   in,   so   out,   so

wide, and he loves me   so. ____
great, _____ ev - ery - where. _
good that it makes me   shout. _

WORDS: Cecilia Olusola Tribble
MUSIC: Cecilia Olusola Tribble

© 2006 Cecilia Olusola Tribble

2   All My Days

In your book were written all the days that were formed for me,
when none of them as yet existed. (Psalm 139:16b)

	1. You	know	my	words,	be -
	(2. If)	I	should	fly	be -
	(3. Our)	ev - ery	thought,	each
	(4. O)	mend	my	heart	and

fore	they're	said.	You	know	my	need	and
yond	the	dawn,	the	dark - ness	will	not
word	we	say,	the	whole	of	time,	the
free	my	voice.	From	sin	re - leased,	I

I	am	fed.	You	give	me	life.	You
o - ver - come.	If	I	lie	down	in
pres - ent	day,	are	held	with - in	your
will	re - joice.	O	search	me,	Lord,	my

know	my	ways,	my strength, my	path,	for
deep - est	night,	still	you	are	there,	my
might - y	hand,	too	won - der - ful	to
spir - it	cries,	and	let	my	song	of

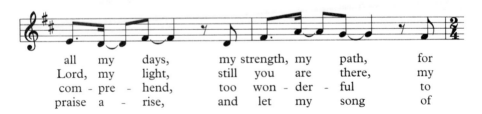

all	my	days,	my strength, my	path,	for
Lord, my	light,	still	you	are	there,	my
com - pre - hend,	too	won - der - ful	to
praise a - rise,	and	let	my	song	of

WORDS: Laurie Zelman
MUSIC: Mark A. Miller

HIXON
88.88

all   my   days. ____

Lord, my   light. ____

com - pre - hend. ____

2. If
3. Our
4. O

praise a - rise _____

Psalm 8: O Lord, How Excellent   3

O LORD, our Sovereign, how majestic is your name in all the earth! (Psalm 8:1a)

O Lord, our Lord, how ex-cel-lent is Thy name.

O   Lord, our Lord, how ex-cel-lent is Thy name.

WORDS: Richard Smallwood (Ps. 8:1)
MUSIC: Richard Smallwood, arr. by Stephen Key

4 Your Great Name We Praise (Immortal, Invisible)

To the King of the ages, immortal, invisible, the only God, be honor and glory
forever and ever. Amen. (1 Timothy 1:17)

1. Im - mor - tal, in - vis - i - ble, God on - ly wise, in
(2. Un) - rest - ing, un - hast - ing, and si - lent as light, nor
(3. All) life comes from you, Lord, to both great and small; in
(4. Great) Fa - ther of glo - ry; pure Fa - ther of light; your

light in - ac - ces - si - ble hid from our eyes, most
want - ing, nor wast - ing, you rule us in might, your
all life you live, Lord, the true life of all; we
an - gels a - dore you, all veil - ing their sight; all

ho - ly, most glo - rious, the An - cient of Days, al -
jus - tice like moun - tains high soar - ing a - bove your
blos - som and flour - ish, but quick - ly grow frail, we
praise we would ren - der: O Fa - ther of grace, 'til

might - y, vic - to - rious, your great name we
clouds which are foun - tains of good - ness and
with - er and per - ish, but you nev - er
one day in splen - dor we see face to

1
praise.

2

2-4
2. Un - love.
fail. }
face. } Most

ho - ly, most glo - ri-ous, the An-cient of Days, al -

WORDS: Walter Chalmers Smith, adapt. by Bob Kauflin
MUSIC: Bob Kauflin

might - y, vic - to - ri-ous, your great name we praise.____

Third time to Coda

2 |1 ||2   D.S.

—   3. All   4. Great

CODA

4

I Lift Up My Hands   5

So I will bless you as long as I live; I will lift up my hands and call on your name. (Psalm 63:4)

Fa - ther,   I   love   you.

My heart is   filled   with de - sire   to   see.   Your

pow - er   and   glo - ry

cov - er   the   earth   as   the   wa - ters clothe the   sea.

I   am sur - round - ed   by the for - tress of   God

WORDS: Israel Houghton and Ricardo Sanchez
MUSIC: Israel Houghton and Ricardo Sanchez, arr. by Linda Furtado and Zeke Listenbee
© 2001 Integrity's Praise! Music/Integrity's Hosanna! Music

to-tal-ly sur-ren - dered to You. __

Pa - dre te a - mo er

mi cor-a-zón. Hay des - e - os de ver Tis

fuer - za tu glo - ri - a que

cu-bre la ti-er-ra co-mo - o - ia del mar.

Soy ro-de-a da de la Gra-cia de Di-os to-tal-

men-te en - tre-ga - da a ti. __ I lift up my hands __

__ stand-ing un - a-shamed __ I wor-ship you, Fa-

ther, ex-alt-ing your name. You've cap-tured my heart, __

6 What a Mighty God We Serve

What god in heaven or on earth can perform deeds and mighty acts like yours! (Deuteronomy 3:24b)

Hal - le - lu, hal - le - lu - jah! Hal - le - lu, hal - le -
lu - jah! Hal - le - lu, hal - le - lu - jah! What a
might - y God we serve. _ Let us sing _
Oh, what a might - y God we serve. _
What a might - y God we serve. _
What a might - y God we serve. _
What a might - y God we
serve! _____

7 Awesome God

And he will reign forever and ever. (Revelation 11:15c)

Our God is an awe-some God, he reigns from

heav-en a-bove with wis - dom, pow'r, and love, our

God is an awe-some God. Our God is an

awe-some God, he reigns from heav-en a-bove with

wis - dom, pow'r, and love, our God is an awe-some God.

He reigns! He reigns! He

WORDS: Richard Mullins
MUSIC: Richard Mullins

AWESOME GOD
Irregular

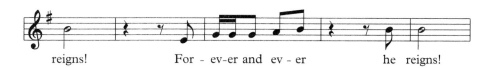

reigns!   For - ev-er and ev - er   he reigns!

He reigns!   He reigns!

Our God   is an awe-some God, he reigns   from

heav-en a - bove with   wis - dom, pow'r, and love, our

God   is an awe - some   God.   Our   God   is an

awe - some God, he   reigns   from   heav-en a - bove with

wis - dom, pow'r, and love, our God is an awe-some God.

8 Almighty

Great and amazing are your deeds, Lord God the Almighty!
Just and true are your ways. (Revelation 15:3b)

1. Let all the earth pro-claim the glo-ry of your name.
(2. All) heav-en lifts you high — the peo-ple tes - ti - fy.

You are still the same Al - might - y. From the
You are Ad - o - nai Al - might - y. — Je-

ris - ing of the sun — 'til the day is done
ho - vah Lord of all, you see the spar - row fall,

you're the Ho - ly One Al - might - y.
hear me when I call, Al - might - y.

Chorus

Won-der-ful Al - might - y God, the great e - ter - nal King.

Mar - vel-ous in all your ways and I will sing your

prais - es, your prais - es. You will al - ways be Al - might-

WORDS: Twila LaBar and Rebecca J. Peck
MUSIC: Twila LaBar and Rebecca J. Peck

9 Bless the Lord

Bless the LORD, O my soul, and all that is within me, bless his holy name. (Psalm 103:1)

WORDS: Psalm 103:1
MUSIC: Andraé Crouch, arr. by Nolan Williams, Jr.
© 1973 Bud John Songs, Inc. (ASCAP), admin. by EMI CMG Publishing

BLESS HIS HOLY NAME
Irregular

Clap Your Hands

Clap your hands, all you peoples; shout to God with loud songs of joy. (Psalm 47:1)

Clap your hands! Clap your hands!

Sing a new song in cel - e - bra - tion!

Clap your hands! Clap your hands!

Sing a new song in cel - e - bra - tion!

Clap your hands! Clap your hands! *Fine*

God is great we praise our God with song! _____

D.C. al Fine

God is great! We praise our God with song! _____

WORDS: Handt Hanson and Paul Murakami
MUSIC: Handt Hanson and Paul Murakami
© 1991 Changing Church Forum

CLAP YOUR HANDS
Irregular

11   Great Jehovah

Hallelujah! For the Lord our God the Almighty reigns. (Revelation 19:6*b*)

WORDS: Colette Coward
MUSIC: Colette Coward

Because of Who You Are

12

Let them give glory to the LORD, and declare his praise in the coastlands. (Isaiah 42:12)

Be - cause of who you are, _____ I give you glo - ry.

Be-cause of who you are, _____ I give you praise. _

Be-cause of who you are, _ I will

lift my voice and say, _ Lord, I wor-ship you be-

cause of who you are. _ Lord, I wor-ship you be-

cause of who you are. _ Be - Je-ho - vah

*Melody is in middle note.

WORDS: Martha D. Munizzi and Daniel S. Munizzi
MUSIC: Martha D. Munizzi and Daniel S. Munizzi

Ji - reh, my pro - vid - er. Je-ho-vah

Nis - si, Lord, you reign in vic-to - ry. Je-ho-vah

Sha - lom, my Prince of Peace, ___ and I wor-

ship you be - cause _ of who you are. ___

Je - ho - vah ___ Je - ho - vah

Ji - reh, my pro - vid - er. Je-ho-vah

Nis - si, Lord, you reign in vic - to -

ry. Je-ho-vah Sha-lom, my Prince of Peace, _

Shout Medley

13   What a Mighty God We Serve

And all the angels … fell on their faces before the throne and worshiped God. (Revelation 7:11)

What a might-y God we serve, _

what a might-y God we serve, _

an-gels bow be-fore him, heav-en and earth a-dore him,

1 what a might-y God we serve. _   **2** —

An-gels bow be-fore him, heav-en and earth a-dore him,

an-gels bow be-fore him, heav-en and earth a-dore him,

1 what a might-y God we serve. _   **2** —

WORDS: Trad. African folk song
MUSIC: Trad. African folk song, arr. by Stephen Key, this arr. by Oscar Dismuke
Arr. © 2000 GIA Publications, Inc.

Shout

My lips will shout for joy when I sing praises to you. (Psalm 71:23a)

So I will shout with a voice of tri - umph,

shout with a voice of praise, _ shout with a voice of tri -

umph, shout with a voice of praise, _

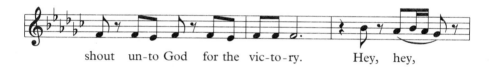

shout un-to God for the vic-to-ry. Hey, hey,

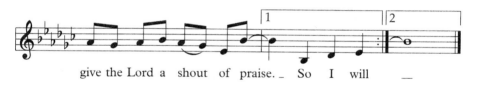

give the Lord a shout of praise. _ So I will _

WORDS: Martha D. Munizzi
MUSIC: Martha D. Munizzi

15 Shout to the Lord

Make a joyful noise to the LORD, all the earth;
break forth into joyous song and sing praises. (Psalm 98:4)

Slow "two"

Shout to the Lord all the earth _ let us sing

pow - er and maj - es - ty, praise _ to the King.

Moun-tains bow down and the seas _ will roar at the

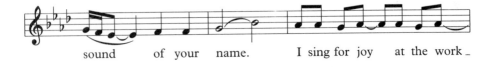

sound of your name. I sing for joy at the work _

_ of your hands, for - ev - er I'll love you, for - ev -

er I'll stand. Noth-ing com - pares to the prom-

ise I have in you.

WORDS: Darlene Zschech
MUSIC: Darlene Zschech, arr. by Oscar Dismuke

ZSCHECH
Irregular

I Worship You, Almighty God/
There is None Like You

16

I am God, and there is no one like me. (Isaiah 46:9b)

I wor-ship you, Al-might-y God; there is none like you. I wor-ship you, O Prince of Peace; that is what I want to do. I give you praise ___ for you are my righ-teous-ness. ___ I wor-ship you, Al-might-y God; there is none like you.

There is none like ___ you, no one else can touch my heart like you do; I could search for all e-ter-ni-ty long and find ___ there is none like ___ you.

*WORDS: Sondra Corbett
MUSIC: Sondra Corbett, arr. by Jonathan Cole Dow

© 1983 Integrity's Hosanna! Music

**WORDS: Lenny Leblanc
MUSIC: Lenny Leblanc

© 1991 Integrity's Hosanna! Music

End of **Shout Medley**

17 God Made Me

God saw everything that God had made, and indeed, it was very good. (Genesis 1:31, alt.)

Chorus (sing twice)
Made heaven and earth, made us from the dirt,
made everything you see from the trees to the church
in one, two, three, four, five, six days
one, two, three, four, five, six, give God praise. (claps)

God made you and God made me
made the heavens and the earth, everything you can see,
all things you can't see, God is so amazing.
Take a look around, God is in everything,
the trees, the plants, the bees, the ants,
the deer, the lions, the seas, the lands.
The ultimate creator gave us a Savior.
Put your hands together, everybody let's praise him.

Gave us fire for heat, gave us air to breathe,
our bodies from the dirt, created human beings,
all things you can see plus God loves me.
Stop, look, and listen, let's praise thee.
Made all the boys and all the girls,
and made me and you and this whole wide world.
God is unfailing, unchanging,
the Creator, let's praise him y'all.

Chorus (two times)

Bridge 1 (sing twice)
Who made me? *God made me.*
Who saved me? *God saved me.*
Amazing, *God's amazing.*
We praise thee, *let's praise thee.*

Bridge 2 (sing twice)
God made me *intelligent.*
God made me *beautiful.*
God made me *smart.*
God made me *capable.*

WORDS: Frederick Burchell
© 2006 B4 Entertainment

Day one, the heavens and the earth was made,
God said, "Let there be light," and the light was day,
and the dark he called night, then God made the sky.
On day two he made the waters divide
and Day three, God made the dry land,
made the grass, the trees, the seeds, and the plants.
Day four, God made the sun and the moon,
the stars, the seasons, saw that it was good.

Day five, God made the fish of all kinds,
but look up high, he made the birds in the sky.
Day six, God created the beasts,
created the cattle and everything that creeps.
But hold on a second, God isn't done yet,
Created human beings in his own image.
The unfailing, unchanging Creator,
let's praise him y'all.

Chorus (sing twice)

Bridge 1 (sing twice)

Bridge 2 (sing twice)

17 God Made Me

God saw everything that God had made, and indeed, it was very good. (Genesis 1:31, alt.)

Chorus
Voice 1

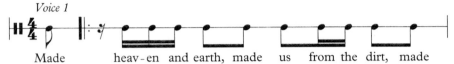

Made heav-en and earth, made us from the dirt, made

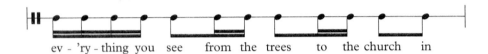

ev - 'ry - thing you see from the trees to the church in

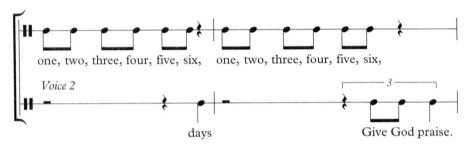

one, two, three, four, five, six, one, two, three, four, five, six,

Voice 2

days Give God praise.

Hand claps

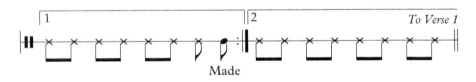

Made

Bridge 1
Voice 1

Who made me? Who saved me?

Voice 2

God made me. God saved me.

WORDS: Frederick Burchell
MUSIC: Frederick Burchell and Kyle Lovett

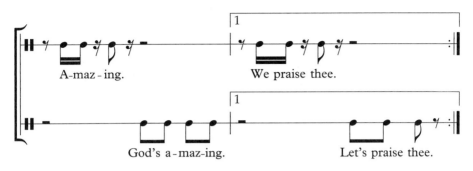

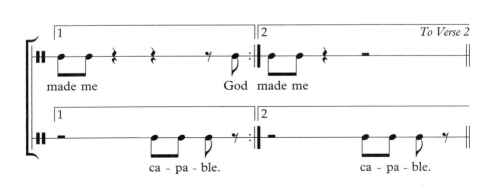

18 God Is Good, All the Time

O give thanks to the LORD, for he is good; for his steadfast love endures forever. (Psalm 107:1)

God is good, God is good all the time. God is good, God is good all the

time.

1. In our doubts, hopes and fears, joys and tears,
2. When there's no one to share our de - spair,
3. When there's love to be found all a - round,
4. When our sor - row we bring, let us sing:
5. As our thanks and our praise now we raise,

God is good, God is good all the time.

WORDS: Dean B. McIntyre
MUSIC: Dean B. McIntyre

GOD IS GOOD
9.9.9.9.

© 2003 Abingdon Press, admin. by The Copyright Co.

19 I Will Bless Thee, O Lord

And now, our God, we give thanks to you and praise your glorious name. (1 Chronicles 29:13)

I will bless thee, O Lord!
up,

I will bless thee, O
and my mouth filled with

Lord!
praise,

With a heart of thanks-giv - ing,
with a heart of thanks-giv - ing,

I will bless thee, O
I will bless thee, O

WORDS: Esther Watanabe
MUSIC: Esther Watanabe, arr. by Nolan Williams, Jr.

© 1970 New Song Music; arr. © 2000 GIA Publications, Inc.

Lord!   With my hands lift - ed   Lord!

I Will Celebrate Medley
I Will Celebrate

20

O sing to the LORD a new song; sing to the LORD, all the earth. (Psalm 96:1)

I   will   praise   him.   I   will sing to him a

new song.   I   will   praise   him.   I   will sing to him a

new song.   I   will cel - e - brate.   Sing un - to the Lord.

I   will sing to him a   new song.   new song.   I   will

praise   him.   I   will sing to him a   new song.   I   will

praise   him.   I   will sing to him a   new   song.

WORDS: Linda Duvall
MUSIC: Linda Duvall, arr. by Cynthia Wilson

21 I Will Sing of the Mercies of the Lord Forever

Let your mercy come to me, that I may live. (Psalm 119:77a)

I will sing of the mer-cies of the Lord for - ev-er. I will

sing. I will sing. I will sing of the mer-cies of the

Lord for - ev - er. I will sing of the mer-cies of the

Lord. With my mouth will I make known thy

faith-ful-ness, thy faith-ful-ness. With my mouth will I make

known thy faith-ful-ness to all gen-er - a - tions. I will

sing of the mer-cies of the Lord for - ev - er. I will

sing. I will sing. I will sing of the mer-cies of the

Lord for - ev - er. I will sing of the mer-cies of the Lord.

WORDS: James H. Fillmore
MUSIC: James H. Fillmore, arr. by Cynthia Wilson

© 2007 Abingdon Press, admin. by The Copyright Co.

I Will Sing unto the Lord

22

"I will sing unto the LORD, for he has triumphed gloriously;
horse and the rider he has thrown into the sea." (Exodus 15:1b)

I will sing un-to the Lord for God has tri-umphed glo-rious-ly, the

horse and the rid - er thrown in - to the sea.

sea.   The   Lord,   my God,   my strength my   song,   has

now   be-come my vic-to - ry.   The   ry.   The

Lord   is   God and   I   will praise God, my   fa - ther's God and

I   will ex - alt   him. The   I   will ex - alt him!

May be sung as a canon.

WORDS: Anon.
MUSIC: Anon., arr. by Cynthia Wilson
Arr. © 2007 Abingdon Press, admin. by The Copyright Co.

End of **I Will Celebrate Medley**

23 A Cause to Celebrate
A Medley of African Gospel Praise Songs

My grace is sufficient for you. (2 Corinthians 12:9a)

*WORDS: Ghanaian praise song
MUSIC: Ghanaian praise song, transcribed and arr. by Newlove Annan

Arr. © 2007 Abingdon Press, admin. by The Copyright Co.

**WORDS: Ghanaian praise song
MUSIC: Ghanaian praise song, transcribed and arr. by Newlove Annan

Arr. © 2007 Abingdon Press, admin. by The Copyright Co.

Glorious

Sing forth the honour of his name; make his praise glorious. (Psalm 66:2 KJV)

When you come in-to his pres-ence lift-ing up the name of Je - sus and you hear the mu - sic play-in' and you see the peo - ple prais - in' just for - get a - bout your wor - ries, get your trou - bles far be - hind you, don't you wait an - oth - er min - ute, just get up and on your feet and get to danc-

WORDS: Martha D. Munizzi and Israel Houghton
MUSIC: Martha D. Munizzi and Israel Houghton

25 Glorious Is the Name of Jesus

Blessed be your glorious name, which is exalted above all blessing and praise. (Nehemiah 9:5b)

Glo - rious is the name of Je - sus, prais - es to his name. Oh, glo - rious and righ - teous and ho - y is his name, Oh, glo - ri - ous is his name. ____ I feel his pres-ence

WORDS: Dr. Robert J. Fryson
MUSIC: Dr. Robert J. Fryson
© 1982 Bob Jay Music Co.

in this place, his Spir - it has con - trol.   Can't you

feel his warm em - brace and all the joy with-in your

soul,   Oh,   glo - ri - ous is his

name, Oh, glo - ri - ous is his name. _____

26 How Majestic Is Your Name

O LORD, our Sovereign, how majestic is your name in all the earth! (Psalm 8:9)

O Lord, our Lord, how ma-jes-tic is your name in all the earth. O earth. O Lord, ___ ___ we praise your name. O Lord, ___ we mag-ni-fy your name: Prince of Peace, Might-y God; O

WORDS: Michael W. Smith
MUSIC: Michael W. Smith
© 1981 Meadowgreen Music Co. (ASCAP), admin. by EMI CMG Publishing

HOW MAJESTIC
Irregular

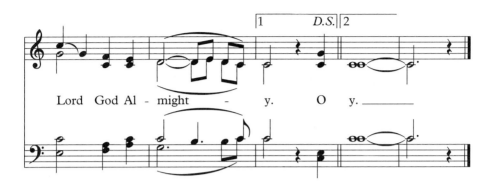

Lord God Al - might - y. O y. ___

Jesus, Name above All Names 27

Therefore God also highly exalted him
and gave him the name that is above every name. (Philippians 2:9)

Je - sus, name a - bove all names, beau - ti - ful

Sav - ior, glo - ri - ous Lord. Em -

man - u - el, God is with us, bless - ed Re -

deem - er, liv - ing Word.

WORDS: Naida Hearn
MUSIC: Naida Hearn

NAME ABOVE ALL NAMES
Irregular

28 I Sing Praises to Your Name

I will be glad and exult in you; I will sing praise to your name. (Psalm 9:2)

1. I sing prais-es to your name, O Lord, prais-es to your name, O Lord, for your name is great and great-ly to be praised; I sing prais-es to your name, O Lord, prais-es to your name, O Lord, for your

2. I give glory to your name ...

WORDS: Terry MacAlmon
MUSIC: Terry MacAlmon

I SING PRAISES
Irregular

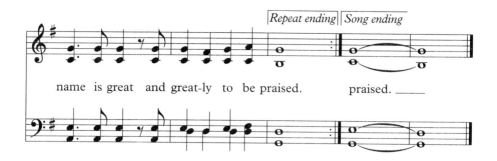

Repeat ending | Song ending

name is great and great-ly to be praised.   praised. _____

Name Medley
Praise the Name of Jesus

29

Lord, who will not fear and glorify your name? (Revelation 15:4a)

Praise the name of Je - sus. Praise the name of Je - sus.

He's my rock; he's my for - tress. He's my de-liv-er-er in

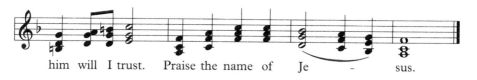

him will I trust. Praise the name of Je - sus.

WORDS: Roy Hicks, Jr.
MUSIC: Roy Hicks, Jr., arr. by Cynthia Wilson
© 1976 Latter Rain Music (ASCAP), admin. by EMI CMG Publishing

HICKS
Irregular

30 Bless That Wonderful Name

"Then everyone who calls on the name of the Lord shall be saved." (Acts 2:21)

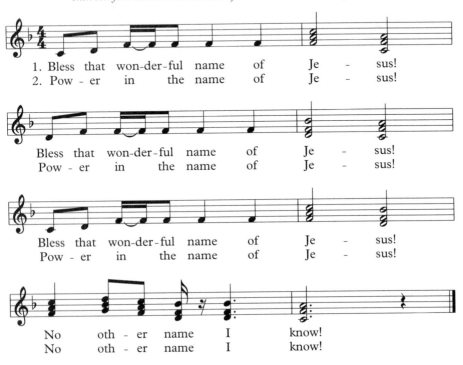

1. Bless that won-der-ful name of Je - sus!
2. Pow - er in the name of Je - sus!

Bless that won-der-ful name of Je - sus!
Pow - er in the name of Je - sus!

Bless that won-der-ful name of Je - sus!
Pow - er in the name of Je - sus!

No oth - er name I know!
No oth - er name I know!

WORDS: Congregational praise song
MUSIC: Congregational praise song, arr. by Cynthia Wilson

Arr. © 2007 Abingdon Press, admin. by The Copyright Co.

31 His Name Is Wonderful

And he is named Wonderful Counselor, Mighty God,
Everlasting Father, Prince of Peace. (Isaiah 9:6b)

His name is won-der-ful! His name is won-der-ful!

His name is won-der-ful! Je - sus my Lord!

WORDS: Audrey Mieir
MUSIC: Audrey Mieir, arr. by Cynthia Wilson

HIS NAME IS WONDERFUL
Irregular

© 1959, renewed 1987 Manna Music, Inc.

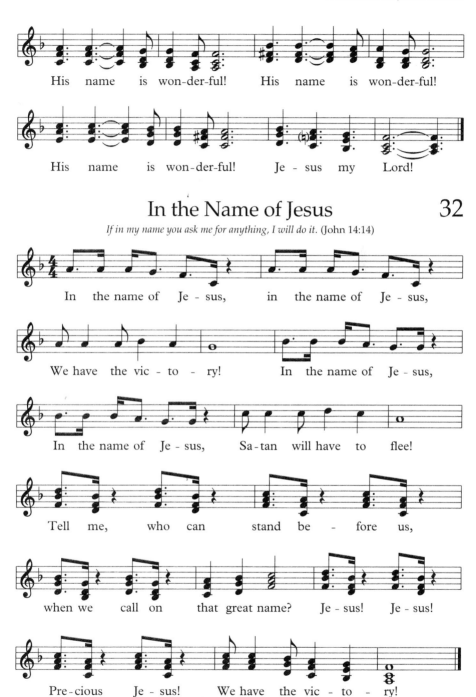

His name is won-der-ful! His name is won-der-ful!

His name is won-der-ful! Je - sus my Lord!

In the Name of Jesus 32

If in my name you ask me for anything, I will do it. (John 14:14)

In the name of Je - sus, in the name of Je - sus,

We have the vic - to - ry! In the name of Je - sus,

In the name of Je - sus, Sa - tan will have to flee!

Tell me, who can stand be - fore us,

when we call on that great name? Je - sus! Je - sus!

Pre - cious Je - sus! We have the vic - to - ry!

WORDS: Congregational praise song
MUSIC: Congregational praise song, arr. by Cynthia Wilson

33 Jesus, What a Beautiful Name

She will bear a son, and you are to name him Jesus,
for he will save his people from their sins. (Matthew 1:21)

1. Je - sus, what a beau-ti-ful name, _____ Son of
2. Je - sus, what a beau-ti-ful name, _____ truth re -
3. Je - sus, what a beau-ti-ful name, _____ res-cued my

God, Son of Man, Lamb that was slain. _____ Joy and
vealed, fu - ture sealed, healed my pain. _____ Love and
soul, my strong-hold, lifts me from shame. _____ For-give-ness,

peace, strength and hope, grace that blows all
free - dom, life and warmth, grace that blows all
se - cu - ri - ty, power, and love, grace that blows all

fear a - way. Je - sus, what a beau-ti-ful
fear a - way. Je - sus, what a beau-ti-ful
fear a - way. Je - sus, what a beau-ti-ful

[1–3] [4]

name. What a beau - ti - ful name.
name.
name.

WORDS: Tanya Riches
MUSIC: Tanya Riches, arr. by Cynthia Wilson

End of **Name Medley**

In the Sanctuary

Lift up your hands to the holy place, and bless the LORD. (Psalm 134:2)

1. We lift our hands in the sanc-tu-ar-y.
2. We clap our hands in the sanc-tu-ar-y.
3. We sing our song in the sanc-tu-ar-y.

We lift our hands to give you the glo-ry.
We clap our hands to give you the glo-ry.
We sing our song to give you the glo-ry.

We lift our hands to give you the praise.
We clap our hands to give you the praise.
We sing our song to give you the praise.

And we will praise you for the rest of our days, Yes,

1, 2 we will praise you for the rest of our days.

3 rest of our days.

Je-sus, we give you the praise, Em-man-u-el, we

lift up your name, Heav-en-ly Fa-ther, com-ing Mes-si-ah,

WORDS: Kurt Carr
MUSIC: Kurt Carr, arr. by Darryl Glenn Nettles

35 Praise Him

The LORD lives! Blessed be my rock, and exalted be my God,
the rock of my salvation. (2 Samuel 22:47)

WORDS: Donnie Harper
MUSIC: Donnie Harper, arr. by Stephen Key

go - ing down of the same, he's wor - thy, Je-sus is

D.C.

wor - thy, he's wor - thy to be praised.

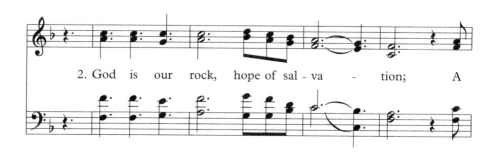

2. God is our rock, hope of sal - va - tion; A

D.C.

strong de - liv-er-er in him will I al-ways trust.

36 The Glory Song
(I'm Gonna Lift You Up)

I glorified you on earth by finishing the work that you gave me to do. (John 17:4)

WORDS: Byron Cage
MUSIC: Byron Cage

37 High Praise

My soul magnifies the Lord, and my spirit rejoices in God my Savior. (Luke 1:47)

Pre-cious, ho-ly bless-ed Sav-ior, you are wor-thy to be praised.

Heav-en and earth bow be-fore you, you are wor-thy to be praised.

Special Chorus*

Pre-cious, ho-ly bless-ed Sav-ior, you are wor-thy to be praised.

Hal - le - lu - jah, hal - le - lu - jah,

Pre-cious, ho-ly bless-ed Sav-ior, hal - le - lu - jah,

Hal - le - lu - jah,

Heav-en and earth bow be-fore you,

Hal - le - lu - jah, you're wor-thy to be praised.

Begin with soprano line, then add each part one at a time

WORDS: Margaret Pleasant Douroux
MUSIC: Margaret Pleasant Douroux

Celebrator

But I will hope continually, and will praise you yet more and more. (Psalm 71:14)

I'm a cel-e-bra-tor   of my cre-a-tor.

Look what God has done.   Sent his on-ly Son

so that I could live,   and I'm gon-na give

my ev-ery-thing.   Ain't God good!   Ain't God good!

Ain't God good!   Ain't God good!

Ain't God good! The   one and on-ly

To repeat

true and Ho-ly   liv-ing God,   liv-ing God.   The

To continue

liv-ing God.   The   one and on-ly   true and Ho-ly

To repeat   *To end*

liv-ing God,   liv-ing God.   The   liv-ing God.

WORDS: Toby Hill, transcribed by Stephanie York Blue
MUSIC: Toby Hill, transcribed by Stephanie York Blue

© 2002 Toby Hill

Love You, Lord, Medley

39 ## I Love You, Lord, Today

For you were bought with a price; therefore glorify God in your body. (1 Corinthians 6:20)

1. I love you, I love you, I
2. My heart, my mind my

love you, Lord, to-day be-cause you care for me in
soul be-longs to you. You paid the price for me way

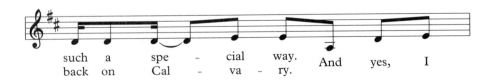

such a spe - cial way. And yes, I
back on Cal - va - ry.

praise you. I lift you up. I mag-ni-fy your name.

That's why my heart is filled with praise.

WORDS: William F. Hubbard
MUSIC: William F. Hubbard
© 1985 Chinwah Songs (SESAC)

I Love You, Lord

I love you, O LORD, my strength. (Psalm 18:1)

I love you, Lord, ___ and I lift my voice ___ to wor - ship you, O my soul re - joice! Take joy, my King, ___ in what you hear ___ may it be a sweet, sweet sound in your ear. ___

WORDS: Laurie Klein
MUSIC: Laurie Klein, arr. by Nolan Williams, Jr.

41 I Really Love the Lord

We love because he first loved us. (1 John 4:19)

WORDS: Jimmy Dowell
MUSIC: Jimmy Dowell, arr. by Nolan Williams, Jr.

© Sound of Gospel; arr. © 2000 GIA Publications, Inc.

End of **Love You, Lord, Medley**

Lord, Reign in Me

And let the peace of Christ rule in your hearts. (Colossians 3:15a)

O-ver all the earth, you reign on high. Ev-'ry moun-tain stream,

ev-'ry sun-set sky. But my one re-quest, Lord, my on-ly aim

is that you'd reign in me a - gain.

O-ver ev-'ry thought, o-ver ev-'ry word, may my life re-flect

WORDS: Brenton Brown
MUSIC: Brenton Brown, arr. by William S. Moon

You are the Lord of all, I am, so won't you reign in me a-gain.

You Inhabit the Praises of Your People 43

But thou art holy, O thou that inhabitest the praises of Israel. (Psalm 22:3 KJV)

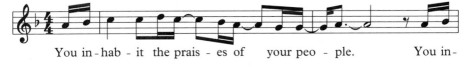

You in-hab-it the prais-es of your peo-ple. You in-

hab-it the prais-es of your peo-ple. We are your peo-

ple, Lord, we praise you. We are your peo-

ple, Lord, we praise you.

WORDS: Regina Hoosier
MUSIC: Regina Hoosier
© 2002 Regina Hoosier (ASCAP)

44

Greater
(I Can Do All Things)

For the one who is in you is greater than the one who is in the world. (1 John 4:4b)

I can do all things through Christ who

strength-ens me. Grace can pull down strong-holds of the

en - e - my. I will stand and fight un - til the

vic - to - ry, for he's great - er. Great-

WORDS: Twila LaBar and Jeff Ferguson
MUSIC: Twila LaBar and Jeff Ferguson

on formed a-gainst me shall pros - per.   He's giv-

en me my shield and my sword. _____   The cham-

pion with-in   me shall con - quer.   Tell me

who can o - ver - come   the Lord. __

I   can   do   all   things through Christ   who

45 And the Word Is God

In the beginning was the Word, and the Word was with God, and the Word was God. (John 1:1)

WORDS: Cecilia Olusola Tribble
MUSIC: Cecilia Olusola Tribble
© 2007 Cecilia Olusola Tribble

46 The Only One

Your word is a lamp to my feet and a light to my path. (Psalm 119:105)

You mean more to me than an-y words could say. ___
You il-lu-mi-nate my path and lead the way. ___
Like a star you shine so bright that I can see ___
your love for me. I nev-er want to live a

WORDS: Antonio Phelon
MUSIC: Antonio Phelon, arr. by William S. Moon

47 Breathe

When he said this, he breathed on them and said to them, "Receive the Holy Spirit." (John 20:22)

This is the air __ I breathe, this is the air __

__ I breathe, your ho - ly pres - ence,

liv - ing in me, __ this is my dai-

ly bread, this is my dai - ly bread,

your ver - y word, _____ spo - ken to me. __

Last time to Coda ⊕

__ And I, _____ I'm des-p'rate for __

__ you. And I, _____

D.C. al Coda

__ I'm lost with-out ____ you.

⊕ **CODA**

I, _____ I'm des-p'rate for ____ you. And

WORDS: Marie Barnett
MUSIC: Marie Barnett, arr. by Mark A. Miller

BREATHE
Irregular

© 1995 Mercy/Vineyard Publishing (ASCAP), admin. in North America by Music Services o/b/o Vineyard Music UK

I, _____ I'm lost with-out ____ you.

To continue _Repeat as desired._

__ you. I'm lost with-out _____ you.

Santo, Santo, Santo 48

Glory in his holy name; let the hearts of those who seek the LORD rejoice. (1 Chronicles 16:10)

¡San - to, san - to, san - to, mi
Ho - ly, ho - ly, ho - ly, my

cor - a - zón te a - do - ra! Mi cor - a - zón te
heart, my heart, a - dores you! My heart is glad to

sa - be de - cir: San - to e - res Se - ñor.
say the words: You are ho - ly, Lord.

WORDS: Argentine folk song
MUSIC: Argentine folk song, arr. by Nolan Williams, Jr.
Arr. © 2000 GIA Publications, Inc.

49   Let It Rise

Arise, shine; for your light has come, and the glory of the LORD has risen upon you. (Isaiah 60:1)

WORDS: Holland Davis
MUSIC: Holland Davis, arr. by Linda Furtado

Show Teeth

*Be glad in the LORD and rejoice, O righteous, and shout for joy,
all you upright in heart. (Psalm 32:11)*

So you say God lives in you and I be-lieve it's

true, so let me see you show yo teeth. Show proof.

You say God lives in you and I be-lieve it's

true, so let me see you show yo teeth. Show proof

Second time to Coda ⊕ *Solo*

1. Tap your neigh - bor on the

shoul - der, ask him what he came here for, and if he re -
(her) (she) (she)

plies, "I wan-na wor-ship God!" then ask if God's been

good, then ask if God has grace. I know God's so real, _

WORDS: Toby Hill
MUSIC: Luke Austin, transcribed by Stephanie York Blue
© 2005 Toby Hill

frown. Are you read-y for this time of fam-'ly glo-ry giv-en to our

Trio

Mak - er, Sup - pli - er, Sus - tain - er of Life? As I

look a - round this room _ I can see God. _

Wo-oo

I can see the mir -

woo - oo woo - oo woo - oo woo - oo woo.

a - cle that's made when you, ___ when you _

Keep on smil - in'.

D.S. al Coda

D.S. al Coda

Keep on smil - in'. You say God lives in

Smile _____ for me. _

So let me see you

Smile _____ for me. -

show yo teeth. Show proof. _

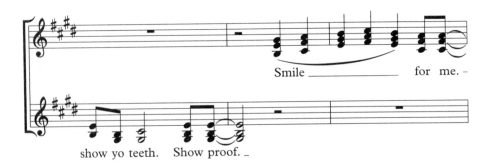

So let me see you show yo teeth. Show proof. _

Smile _____ for me. _

So let me see you

51 Wailing into Dancing

You have turned my mourning into dancing;
you have taken off my sackcloth and clothed me with joy. (Psalm 30:11)

WORDS: Donn Thomas
MUSIC: Donn Thomas, transcribed by William S. Moon

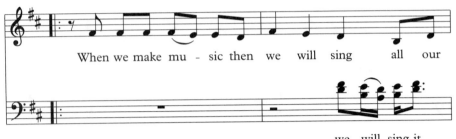

When we make mu - sic then we will sing all our

we will sing it

foun - tains are found in you. ____

are found in you.

We'll praise your name, Lord, when we're danc - ing,

we're danc - ing

1

2

tam-bou-rine, harp, and flute. flute. You turned my

way. You turned my wail-ing in-to danc-ing, took a-

way my sad-ness and gave me joy.

You made my heart sing, I can't keep si-lent, I will

Sing three times

give you praise for-ev-er-more. I will

give you praise for-ev-er-more.

52 Incredible

For to me, living is Christ and dying is gain. (Philippians 1:21)

Oh, oh, oh, oh, oh, oh, ah, ah, ah. Oh, oh, oh,

oh, oh, oh, ah, ah, ah. _____ ah. _____ 1. I found an-oth-er

(Verse 1)

life to lead ___ be - yond what car-nal minds con-ceive.

(Verse 2)

have to run, ___ and I al-ways seem to o - ver-come

I die to what I think I need

as though my bat-tles have al - read - y been won.

on-ly to be blessed more a - bun - dant-ly.

Now life is a game I play just for fun.

WORDS: Brian C. Wilson
MUSIC: Brian C. Wilson and Leon C. Lewis

53 All Hail King Jesus

"It is I, Jesus … I am the root and the descendant of David,
the bright morning star." (Revelation 22:16)

All hail King Je - sus! All hail Em-man - u - el, ____
____ King of kings, Lord of lords, bright Morn-ing
Star. ____ And through-out e-ter - ni - ty, I'll sing your
prais - es; ____ and I'll reign with you through-out e-ter - ni -

WORDS: Dave Moody
MUSIC: Dave Moody
© 1978 Dayspring Music, LLC

KING JESUS
Irregular

ty. _____ All hail King ty. _____ And through ty. _____

He Came Down 54

He came to what was his own … but to all who received him …
he gave power to become children of God. (John 1:11-12)

He came down that we may have *love; he

came down that we may have love; he came down that we may

have love, hal-le-lu-jah for-ev-er-more. Why did he come?

Substitute peace, joy, hope, life, etc.

WORDS: Cameroon traditional
MUSIC: Cameroon traditional; trans. and arr. by John L. Bell

55 Already Here

The LORD is in his holy temple. (Psalm 11:4a)

Group 1: We watch and we wait, Lord, we an-ti-ci-pate the mo-ment you choose to ap-pear. We wor-ship, we praise un-til there's no de-bate and we re-cog-nize you're al-read-y here.

Group 2 (on repeat only): ia.

Group 2: Al — le — lu — ia. You're al-read-y here. Al — le —

WORDS: Brian C. Wilson
MUSIC: Brian C. Wilson, transcribed by Stephanie York Blue

© Brian C. Wilson

56 Amen Siakudumisa

All the people answered, "Amen, Amen."
Then they bowed their heads and worshiped the LORD. (Nehemiah 8:6)

WORDS: Trad. Xhosa (South Africa); attr. to S. C. Molefe as taught by George Mxadana MASITHI
MUSIC: Trad. Xhosa melody, as taught by George Mxadana, arr. by John L. Bell Irregular

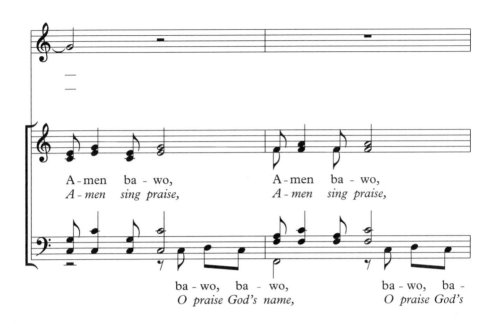

A - men ba - wo,   A - men ba - wo,
A - men sing praise,   *A - men sing praise,*

ba - wo, ba - wo,   ba - wo, ba -
O praise God's name,   *O praise God's*

(Omit last time.)

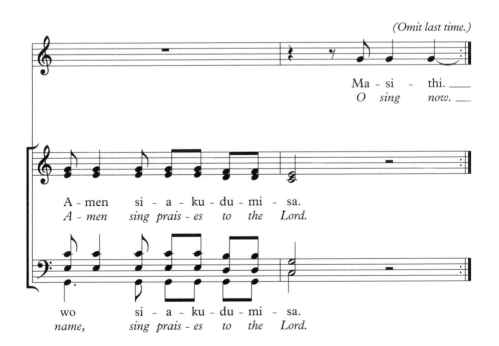

Ma - si - thi. ____
O sing now. ___

A - men si - a - ku - du - mi - sa.
A - men sing prais - es to the Lord.

wo   si - a - ku - du - mi - sa.
name,   *sing prais - es to the Lord.*

57 Emmanuel

And they shall name him Emmanuel, which means, "God is with us." (Matthew 1:23b)

Come, _____ come let us a - dore him, _____ kneel down be -

fore him, wor-ship and a - dore him. _____

Come, _____ come let us a - dore him, _____ kneel down be -

fore him, wor - ship and a - dore him.

Em - man - u - el, Em - man - u - el,

Em - man - u - el, Em - man - u - el,

WORDS: Norman Hutchins
MUSIC: Norman Hutchins and Jason White

Em - man-u-el, Em-man-u-el,

Em-man - u-el, Em-man - u-el,

Em - man-u-el, Em-man-u-el,

Em-man - u-el, Em-man - u-el,

we wor-ship you, we wor-ship you.

Bethlehem

In the time of King Herod … Jesus was born in Bethlehem of Judea. (Matthew 2:1a)

Beth - le - hem, _ Beth - le - hem, _ cit - y where _

_ the King was born. _ Beth - le - hem, _

Beth - le - hem, _ Ma - ry had - a Je - sus on

Fine

Christ-mas morn. _
1. Ma - ry, Ma - ry, meek and mild; _
2. Jo-seph took Ma - ry by the hand,
3. Ma - ry put Je - sus in the hay. _

Ma - ry had - a Je - sus on Christ-mas morn. _
Ma - ry had - a Je - sus on Christ-mas morn. _
Ma - ry had - a Je - sus on Christ-mas morn. _

Moth - er of _ the Ho - ly Child; _
Trav - el - ing _ through - out the land. _
That was his bed _ on Christ - mas Day. _

D.C. al Fine

Ma - ry had - a Je - sus on Christ-mas morn. _
Ma - ry had - a Je - sus on Christ-mas morn. _
Ma - ry had - a Je - sus on Christ-mas morn. _

WORDS: Marilyn E. Thornton
MUSIC: Marilyn E. Thornton

59 Go, Tell It on the Mountain

When they saw this, they made known what had been told them about this child. (Luke 2:17)

Go, tell it on the moun-tain, o-ver the hills and ev - ery-where.

Fine

Go, tell it on the moun - tain that Je - sus Christ is born.

1. Oh, when I was a seek - er, I sought both night and day.
2. While shep-herds kept their watch-ing o'er si - lent flocks by night,
3. The shep-herds feared and trem-bled, when lo! a - bove the earth,
4. Down in a low - ly man-ger the hum - ble Christ was born,

D.C.

I asked the Lord to help me, and he showed me the way.
be - hold through-out the heav-ens there shone a ho - ly light.
rang out the an - gel cho-rus that hailed the Sav - ior's birth.
and God sent us sal - va - tion that bless - ed Christ-mas morn.

WORDS: African American spiritual, adapt. by John W. Work
MUSIC: African American spiritual, arr. by William S. Moon
Arr. © 2007 Abingdon Press, admin. by The Copyright Co.

GO TELL IT ON THE MOUNTAIN
Irregular with Refrain

The Virgin Mary Had a Baby Boy

60

The virgin's name was Mary. (Luke 1:27b)

WORDS: West Indian carol
MUSIC: West Indian carol, arr. by John Barnard

THE VIRGIN MARY
10 10.10 9 with Refrain

61 Heaven's Christmas Tree

Then the angel showed me the river of the water of life. …
On either side of the river, is the tree of life. (Revelation 22:1-2a)

1. I have heard of a tree, a great Christ-mas tree, it was
2. There is one I be-hold in let-ters of gold, It
3. There is one just a-bove, it's ti-tle is love, it is
4. An-oth-er I see, it must be for me, the
5. There are man-y I'm sure, but just this one more I

stall.
me.
stain.
read.
rest.

fixed in yon Beth-le-hem's, Beth-le-hem's stall. The
hangs on a limb near to, limb near to me. 'Tis
marked by a deep crim-son, deep crim-son stain. For
words "I will help you" I, help you I read. While
speak of a-bove all the, bove all the rest. It

bless-ings of heav-en for you and for me, a
la-beled "sal-va-tion," and Je-sus, I'm told, has
there it was tied by the Lord when he died, and
hold-ing his hand, by faith I can stand, and
spells "hap-py home" with God near the throne, a

WORDS: Charles A. Tindley
MUSIC: Charles A. Tindley, arr. by Charles A. Tindley, Jr.

HEAVEN'S CHRISTMAS TREE
11 9 11 7 with Refrain

Christ - mas pres - ent for all.
bought that pack - age for me.
glo - ry to his dear name.
this is the pack - age I need.
place where the wea - ry shall rest.

There is a pack - age for me on that tree; a

pre - cious to - ken that some - one loves me. Oh yes, I can see on

Cal - va - ry's Tree, that there is a pack - age for me.

62 Jesus, the Light of the World

Again Jesus spoke to them, saying, "I am the light of the world." (John 8:12a)

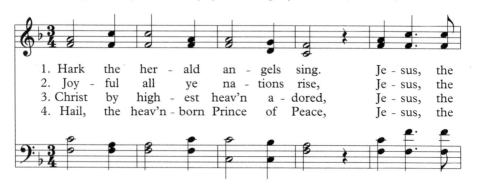

1. Hark the her - ald an - gels sing. Je - sus, the
2. Joy - ful all ye na - tions rise, Je - sus, the
3. Christ by high - est heav'n a - dored, Je - sus, the
4. Hail, the heav'n - born Prince of Peace, Je - sus, the

light of the world. _____ Glo - ry to the
light of the world. _____ Join the tri - umph
light of the world. _____ Christ, the ev - er -
light of the world. _____ Hail, the Sun of

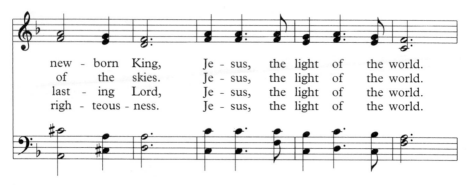

new - born King, Je - sus, the light of the world.
of the skies. Je - sus, the light of the world.
last - ing Lord, Je - sus, the light of the world.
righ - teous - ness. Je - sus, the light of the world.

WORDS: George D. Elderkin, stanzas by Charles Wesley
MUSIC: George D. Elderkin, arr. by Evelyn Simpson-Currenton, alt.
Arr. © 2000, 2007 GIA Publications, Inc.

WE'LL WALK IN THE LIGHT
7 7 7 7 with Refrain

We'll   walk   in   the light,   beau - ti - ful

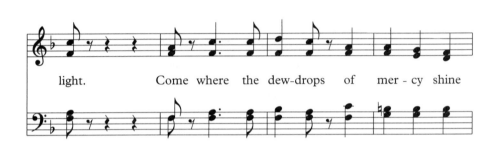

light.   Come where the dew-drops of   mer - cy shine

bright.   Shine   all   a - round us   by   day and by

night.   Je - sus,   the   light   of   the world.

63 Star-Child

For we observed his star at its rising, and have come to pay him homage. (Matthew 2:2b)

1. Star - Child   earth - Child   go - be - tween   of   God,
2. Street child,   beat child,   no place left   to   go,
3. Grown child,   old child,   mem-ory full   of   years,
4. Spared child,   spoiled child,   hav - ing, want - ing   more,
5. Hope - for - peace Child,   God's stu - pen - dous   sign,

love Child,   Christ Child,   heav-en's light - ning   rod,
hurt child,   used child,   no one wants   to   know,
sad child,   lost child,   sto - ry told   in   tears,
wise child,   faith child,   know-ing joy   in   store,
down - to - earth Child,   Star of stars   that   shine,

This year,   this year,   let the day   ar - rive   when

Christ-mas comes for   ev - ery-one,   ev - ery-one   a - live!

WORDS: Shirley Erena Murray
MUSIC: Carlton R. Young
© 1994 Hope Publishing Co.

STAR CHILD
45.45 with Refrain

Epiphany

And they knelt down and paid him homage.
Then, opening their treasure chests, they offered him gifts. (Matthew 2:11)

1. Wis-dom from a - far, __ guid - ed by a star; __
2. Light of our dark night, _ give us ho - ly sight. _
3. Called to do your will, _ Lord, we seek you still. __

— Christ up - on the earth, _
— Lord, we seek your face, __
— Calm our trem - bling fears __

giv - ing all new birth. _ Joy - ful let our spir -
grant us all your grace. _ Hum - bly now our songs
that we may draw near. _ Lead us, Sav - ior, till

its soar, joined to praise you and a - dore.
we raise, of - fering hearts of love and praise.
we stand safe with you in heav - en's land.

WORDS: Gennifer Benjamin Brooks
MUSIC: William S. Moon

65 He Is the Son of God

Truly, this man was God's Son. (Matthew 27:54b)

Claps (Verses 1 and 4)

1. I wan-na tell you a-bout Je - sus, the
(4.) told you a-bout Je - sus, the

(Verse 2)

(2.) walked on the wa-ter,

(Verse 3)

(3.) fed five thou-sand peo - ple,

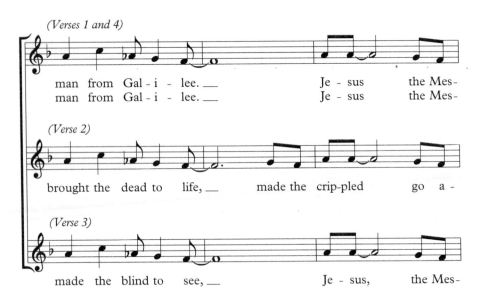

(Verses 1 and 4)

man from Gal - i - lee. ___ Je - sus the Mes-
man from Gal - i - lee. ___ Je - sus the Mes-

(Verse 2)

brought the dead to life, ___ made the crip-pled go a -

(Verse 3)

made the blind to see, ___ Je - sus, the Mes-

WORDS: Marilyn E. Thornton
MUSIC: Marilyn E. Thornton

© 1995 Marilyn E. Thornton

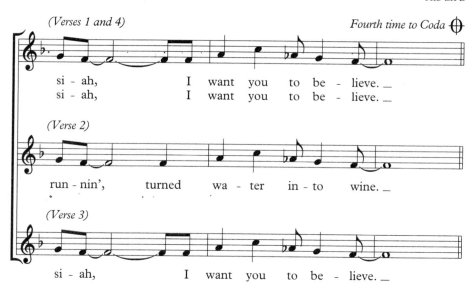

si - ah,   I   want   you   to   be - lieve. __
si - ah,   I   want   you   to   be - lieve. __

run - nin',   turned   wa - ter   in - to   wine. __

si - ah,   I   want   you   to   be - lieve. __

He   is   the   Son   of   God. __

2. He   4. Now I've
3. He

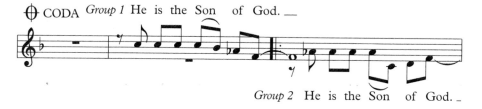

Group 1   He   is   the   Son   of   God. __

Group 2   He   is   the   Son   of   God. _

He   is   the   Son   of   God. __

66 Yield Not to Temptation

Blessed is anyone who endures temptation. (James 1:12a)

1. Yield not to temp-ta-tion, for yield-ing is sin;
2. Shun e-vil com-pan-ions, bad lan-guage dis-dain;
3. To him** that o'er-com-eth, God giv-eth a crown;

each vic-t'ry will help you some oth-er to win;
God's name hold in rev-erence, nor take it in vain;
Thro' faith we will con-quer, tho' of-ten cast down;

fight man-ful-ly* on-ward, dark pas-sions sub-due;
be thought-ful and ear-nest, kind-heart-ed and true;
he who is our Sav-ior, our strength will re-new;

look ev-er to Je-sus, he'll car-ry you through.
look ev-er to Je-sus, he'll car-ry you through.
look ev-er to Je-sus, he'll car-ry you through.

Refrain

Ask the Sav-ior to help you, com-fort, strength-en, and keep you;

he is will-ing to aid you, he will car-ry you through.

"valiantly" may be substituted for "manfully"
**"those" may be substituted for "him"*

WORDS: Horatio Richmond Palmer
MUSIC: Horatio Richmond Palmer

YIELD NOT
65 65 66 66 with Refrain

At the Cross

*But God proves his love for us
in that while we still were sinners Christ died for us.* (Romans 5:8)

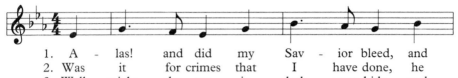

1. A - las! and did my Sav - ior bleed, and
2. Was it for crimes that I have done, he
3. Well might the sun in dark - ness hide, and
4. But drops of grief can ne'er re - pay the

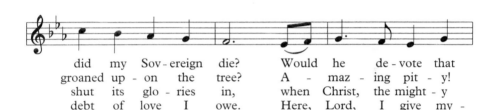

did my Sov - ereign die? Would he de - vote that
groaned up - on the tree? A - maz - ing pit - y!
shut its glo - ries in, when Christ, the might - y
debt of love I owe. Here, Lord, I give my -

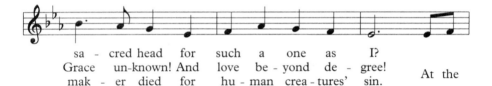

sa - cred head for such a one as I?
Grace un-known! And love be - yond de - gree!
mak - er died for hu - man crea - tures' sin.
self a - way; 'tis all that I can do.

At the

cross, at the cross, where I first saw the light, and the

bur-den of my heart rolled a - way; it was there by faith I re -

ceived my sight, and now I am hap-py all the day.

WORDS: Isaac Watts and Ralph E. Hudson
MUSIC: Ralph E. Hudson, arr. by Oscar Dismuke
Arr. © 2007 Abingdon Press, admin. by The Copyright Co.

HUDSON
CM with Refrain

68 God Weeps

For these things I weep; my eyes flow with tears …
my children are desolate, for the enemy has prevailed. (Lamentations 1:16)

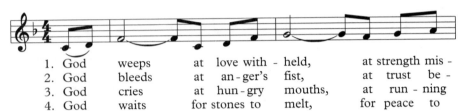

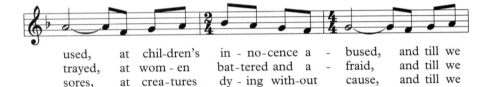

1. God weeps at love with - held, at strength mis -
2. God bleeds at an - ger's fist, at trust be -
3. God cries at hun - gry mouths, at run - ning
4. God waits for stones to melt, for peace to

used, at chil-dren's in - no-cence a - bused, and till we
trayed, at wom - en bat-tered and a - fraid, and till we
sores, at crea-tures dy - ing with-out cause, and till we
seed, for hearts to hold each oth-er's need, and till we

change the way we love, God weeps.
change the way we win, God bleeds.
change the way we care, God cries.
un - der-stand the Christ, God waits.

WORDS: Shirley Erena Murray
MUSIC: Mark A. Miller
DAKE
64.8 10
Words © 1996 Hope Publishing Company; music © 2007 Abingdon Press, admin. by The Copyright Co.

69 I Want Jesus to Walk with Me

"I will live in them and walk among them, and I will be their God,
and they shall be my people." (2 Corinthians 6:16b)

1. _ I want Je - sus _____ to walk with me; _____
2. _ In my tri - als, _____ Lord, walk with me; _____
3. When I'm in trou - ble, _____ Lord walk with me; _____

WORDS: Trad. African American
MUSIC: Trad. African American
SOJOURNER
88 8 9

I want Je - sus ____ to walk with me; ____
In my tri - als, ____ Lord, walk with me; ____
when I'm in trou - ble, ____ Lord, walk with me; ____

all a - long my ____ pil - grim jour - ney, __
when my heart is ____ al - most break - ing, __
when my head is ____ bowed in sor - row, __

Lord, I want Je - sus ____ to walk with me. ____
Lord, I want Je - sus ____ to walk with me. ____
Lord, I want Je - sus ____ to walk with me. ____

O Lord, Fix Me 70

Lord, if you choose, you can make me clean. (Matthew 8:2b)

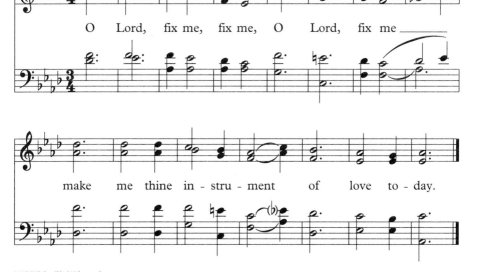

Very slowly

O Lord, fix me, fix me, O Lord, fix me ____

make me thine in - stru - ment of love to - day.

WORDS: Eli Wilson, Jr.
MUSIC: Eli Wilson, Jr.

71 Nothing Between

For I am convinced that neither death, nor ... anything else in all creation,
will be able to separate us from the love of God in Christ Jesus our Lord. (Romans 8:38-39)

1. Noth-ing be-tween my soul and the Sav-ior, naught of this world's de-lu-sive dream: I have re-nounced all sin-ful plea-sure,
2. Noth-ing be-tween like world-ly plea-sure, hab-its of life tho' harm-less they seem, must not my heart from him ev-er sev-er,
3. Noth-ing be-tween like pride or sta-tion: self or friends shall not in-ter-vene; tho' it may cost me much trib-u-la-tion,
4. Noth-ing be-tween e'en man-y hard tri-als, tho' the whole world a-gainst me con-vene; watch-ing with prayer and much self-de-ni-al,

WORDS: Charles A. Tindley
MUSIC: Charles A. Tindley
Arr. © 1979 J. Edward Hoy

NOTHING BETWEEN
10 9 10 9 with Refrain

Je - sus is mine, there's noth - ing be - tween.
he is my all! There's noth - ing be - tween.
I am re - solved! There's noth - ing be - tween.
tri - umph at last, with noth - ing be - tween.

Refrain

Noth-ing be-tween my soul and the Sav-ior, so that his bless - ed face may be seen; noth - ing pre - vent-ing the least of his fa - vor: keep the way clear! Let noth-ing be-tween.

72 He Will Remember Me

Then he said, "Jesus, remember me when you come into your kingdom." (Luke 23:42)

1. When on the cross of Cal-vary the Lord was cru - ci - fied;
2. O, what a shame to kill him there on that rug-ged cross;
3. At his dear feet I'm kneel-ing, my sins I now con - fess;

the mob stood 'round a - bout him and mocked un - til he died.
but such a death was need-ed to res - cue all the lost.
I bow in deep re - pen-tance, my soul he'll sure-ly bless.

Two thieves were nailed be - side him to share the ag - o - ny,
His blood was made a ran-som to set the cap-tives free,
My blind - ed eyes he o - pens so that the light I see,

but one of them cried out to him, "O Lord re-mem-ber me."
I know that I'm in - clud-ed, and he will re-mem-ber me.
and when I reach the pearl-y gates, he will re-mem-ber me.

WORDS: Eugene M. Bartlett
MUSIC: Eugene M. Bartlett, arr. by Nolan Williams, Jr.
Arr. © 1976, renewed 2004 Albert E. Brumley & Sons, admin. by ICG

REMEMBER ME
76.76.76.86 with Refrain

73

Calvary

And when they were come to the place, which is called Calvary,
there they crucified him. (Luke 23:33a KJV)

Cal - va - ry, _____ Cal - va - ry, Cal - va -

ry, _____ Cal - va - ry, Cal - va - ry, _____ Cal - va -

Fine

ry, _____ sure - ly he died on _____ Cal - va - ry. _____

WORDS: African American spiritual
MUSIC: African American spiritual

CALVARY
LM with Refrain

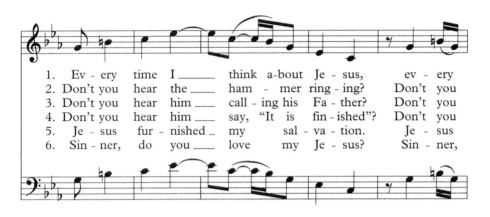

1. Ev - ery time I ____ think a-bout Je - sus, ev - ery
2. Don't you hear the ____ ham - mer ring - ing? Don't you
3. Don't you hear him ____ call - ing his Fa - ther? Don't you
4. Don't you hear him ____ say, "It is fin - ished"? Don't you
5. Je - sus fur - nished _ my sal - va - tion. Je - sus
6. Sin - ner, do you ____ love my Je - sus? Sin - ner,

time I ____ think a-bout Je - sus, ____ ev - ery time I ____
hear the ____ ham - mer ring - ing? ____ Don't you hear the ____
hear him ____ call - ing his Fa - ther? ____ Don't you hear him ____
hear him ____ say, "It is fin - ished"? _ Don't you hear him ____
fur - nished _ my sal - va - tion. ____ Je - sus fur - nished _
do you ____ love my Je - sus? ____ Sin - ner, do you ____

D.C.

_ think a-bout Je - sus, ____ sure - ly he died on __ Cal - va - ry.
_ ham - mer ring - ing? ____ Sure - ly he died on __ Cal - va - ry.
_ call - ing his Fa - ther? ____ Sure - ly he died on __ Cal - va - ry.
_ say, "It is fin - ished"? _ Sure - ly he died on __ Cal - va - ry.
_ my sal - va - tion. ____ Sure - ly he died on __ Cal - va - ry.
_ love my Je - sus? ____ Sure - ly he died on __ Cal - va - ry.

74 Lamb of God

"Here is the Lamb of God who takes away the sin of the world!" (John 1:29)

1. Your on - ly Son, no sin to hide, but you have
(2. Your gift of) love they cru - ci - fied, they laughed and
(3. I was so) lost I should have died but you have

sent him from your side to walk up - on this guilt - y
scorned him as he died: The hum-ble King they named a
brought me to your side to be led by your staff and

sod, and to be - come the Lamb of God. 2. Your gift of
fraud, and sac - ri - ficed the Lamb of
rod, and to be called a lamb of

WORDS: Twila Paris
MUSIC: Twila Paris

LAMB OF GOD
LM with Refrain

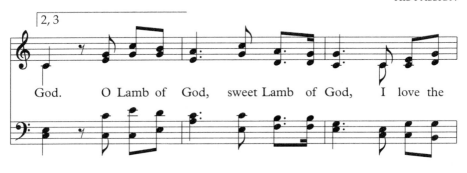

God. O Lamb of God, sweet Lamb of God, I love the

ho - ly Lamb of God! O wash me in his pre-cious

blood, my Je - sus Christ, the Lamb of

Repeat ending   *Song ending*

God.   3. I was so   God. _____

75 The Lamb

"To the one seated on the throne and to the Lamb
be blessing and honor and glory and might forever and ever!" (Revelation 5:13b)

1. Hal-le - lu - jah to the Lamb of God; Hal-le -
2. ___ Ho - ly is the Lamb of God; ___
3. ___ Wor-thy is the Lamb of God; ___
4. ___ Je - sus, you're the Lamb of God; ___

lu - jah to the Lamb of God;
Ho - ly is the Lamb of God;
Wor - thy is the Lamb of God;
Je - sus, you're the Lamb of God;
We

bow down be-fore you; we wor-ship and a-dore you.
Hal-le -
___
___

lu - jah to the Lamb of God. __
Ho - ly is the Lamb of God. __
Wor - thy is the Lamb of God. __
Je - sus, you're the Lamb of God. __
The

per - fect sac - ri-fice you are.
The

great - est gift in life by far.
In

WORDS: Michael McKay
MUSIC: Michael McKay, arr. by William S. Moon

hum - ble grat - i - tude   I   come. _   Hal-le -

lu - jah to   the   Lamb   of   God. __

Halle, Halle, Halleluja   76

"I am the resurrection and the life.
Those who believe in me, even though they die, will live." (John 11:25)

Hal - le, hal - le, hal - le - lu - ja.
1. I AM the Rock of A - ges   cleft for me;
2. I AM the Noth-ing in __ my   hands I bring;
3. I AM the Bread of Life, ___   feed on me;
4. I AM the Res - ur - rec - tion, live in me;

Hal - le, hal - le, hal - le - lu - ja.
I AM the let me hide my-self   in   thee;
I AM the Sim - ply to __ thy   cross I cling;
I AM the One True Vine, ___   grow in me.
I AM the Way, the Truth, ___   fol - low me;

Hal - le, hal - le, hal - le - lu - ja.
I AM the Rock of A - ges   cleft for me;
I AM the Noth-ing in __ my   hands I bring; ⎫ Hal - le -
I AM the Bread of Life, ___   feed on me; ⎬
I AM the Res - ur - rec - tion, live in me; ⎭

1-4   Final

lu - ja, hal - le - lu - ja. _____   ja. __

WORDS: George Mulrain, Trinidad and Tobago
MUSIC: Caribbean folk song; arr. by Carlton R. Young
Sts. 1–4 words and arr. © 1995 General Board of Global Ministries, GBGMusik.

HALLE, HALLE
Irregular

77 Raised, He's Been Raised from the Dead

"Why do you look for the living among the dead? He is not here, but has risen." (Luke 24:5b)

Raised,   he's   been   raised from   the   dead.

Raised,   he's   been   raised from   the   dead.

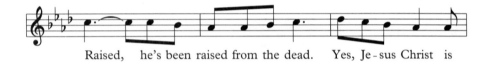

Raised,   he's been raised from the dead.   Yes, Je-sus Christ is

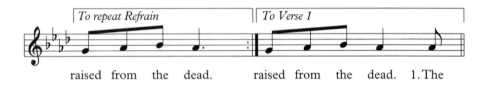

To repeat Refrain   *To Verse 1*

raised from   the   dead.   raised from   the   dead.   1. The

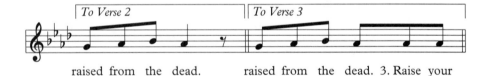

To Verse 2   *To Verse 3*

raised from   the   dead.   raised from   the   dead. 3. Raise your

Verse 1

grave   no long-er   holds him;   the   tomb,   it   can-not

hide him;   and death can no more claim him;   yes, Je-sus Christ is

WORDS: Gennifer Benjamin Brooks
MUSIC: Monya Davis Logan

Words © 2007 Gennifer Benjamin Brooks; music © 2007 Monya Davis Logan

To Refrain

raised from the dead. Oh, yes, Je-sus Christ is raised from the dead.

Verse 2

2. Sin and sor-row lost their sway. An-gels rolled the stone a -

way. Christ, our Lord, is risen to - day.

Yes, Je - sus Christ is raised from the dead. Oh,

To Refrain

yes, Je - sus Christ is raised from the dead.

Verse 3

ban-ner, join the throng, fol-low Christ your whole life

long Al-le - lu-ia, raise the song. Yes, Je-sus Christ is

Repeat as desired.

raised from the dead. Oh, yes, Je-sus Christ is raised from the dead.

78 Friend

"When the Advocate comes, whom I will send to you from the Father,
the Spirit of truth … he will testify on my behalf." (John 15:26)

Ho-ly Spir-it, Ho-ly Ghost, Com-fort-er, Teach-er,

Par-a-clete, Me-di-a-tor, Ad-vo-cate, Re-mind-er.

Some call you Ho-ly Spir-it, some say Ho-ly Ghost, but I

love to call you Friend. _____

WORDS: Helena Barrington
MUSIC: Helena Barrington, transcribed by William S. Moon

© 1993 Integrity's Praise! Music

79 Your Power

"But you will receive power when the Holy Spirit has come upon you." (Acts 1:8a)

1. __ You made __ me for your glo - ry, you plant-
(2. See there is) _____ a roam - ing li - on, who roars _

ed ev - ery seed, _ they are grow - ing in - to sto-
__ to make me fear, _ to re-mind _ me of my fail-

WORDS: Brian C. Wilson
MUSIC: Brian C. Wilson and Leon C. Lewis

Words © 2003 Brian C. Wilson; music © 2003 Brian C. Wilson and Leon C. Lewis

Holy Spirit Medley
Holy Spirit

80

"But you will receive power when the Holy Spirit has come upon you." (Acts 1:8a)

We need the pow-er of the Ho-ly Spir - it, Ho-ly Spir - it,

Send your a - noint-ing. Let it fall down, fall down,

fall down, down on me. —

WORDS: Richard Smallwood
MUSIC: Richard Smallwood, arr. by Nolan Williams, Jr.

81 Let Your Spirit Come

"In the last days it will be, God declares,
that I will pour out my Spirit upon all flesh." (Acts 2:17a)

WORDS: John Chisum
MUSIC: John Chisum

Come and wash us now, come and

wash us now, come and wash us whole

wash us whole. Let your Spir - it come,

Let your Spir - it come, fall up -

fall up - on us now. Let your

on us now; Let your Spir - it come,

Spir - it come, fall up - on us now.

fall up - on us now; fall up - on us now.

82   The Presence of the Lord Is Here

Tremble, O earth, at the presence of the LORD, at the presence of the God of Jacob. (Psalm 114:7)

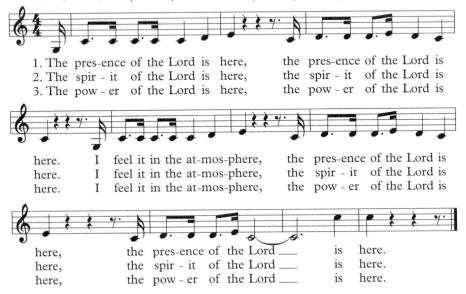

1. The pres-ence of the Lord is here,   the pres-ence of the Lord is
2. The spir - it of the Lord is here,   the spir - it of the Lord is
3. The pow - er of the Lord is here,   the pow - er of the Lord is

here.   I   feel it in the at-mos-phere,   the pres-ence of the Lord is
here.   I   feel it in the at-mos-phere,   the spir - it of the Lord is
here.   I   feel it in the at-mos-phere,   the pow - er of the Lord is

here,   the pres-ence of the Lord ___ is here.
here,   the spir - it of the Lord ___ is here.
here,   the pow - er of the Lord ___ is here.

Four-part choral parts with section "Everybody blow the trumpet" appear in the accompaniment edition.

WORDS: Kurt Carr
MUSIC: Kurt Carr

© 2003 Lilly Mack Music, K Cartunes, admin. by Lilly Mack Music

End of **Holy Spirit Medley**

83   Praise God, from Whom All Blessings Flow

Praise the LORD! How good it is to sing praise to our God; for he is gracious. (Psalm 147:1)

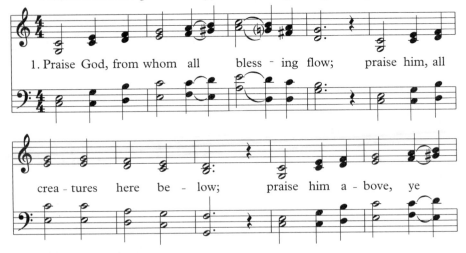

1. Praise God, from whom all   bless - ing flow;   praise him, all

crea - tures here be - low;   praise him a - bove, ye

WORDS: Thomas Ken, adapt. Isaac Watts and William Kethe
MUSIC: Adapt. John Hatton, by George Coles, arr. by Roberta Martin

© 1968 Roberta Martin

heav - en - ly host;   praise Fa-ther, Son, and   Ho - ly   Ghost.

2. Peo - ple and realms of   ev - 'ry   tongue,   dwell on his
3. Sing to the Lord with   cheer - ful   voice,   come ye be -

love with sweet - est song,   to   him shall end - less
fore him and re - joice,   all   peo - ple that on

prayer be made,   and end - less prais - es   crown his
earth   do dwell,   serve him with mirth, his   prais - es

1 · · 2 · · · · Sing two times

head.   tell.   A - men,   A - men.

84 Give Me Jesus

For to me, living is Christ and dying is gain. (Galatians 1:21)

1. I heard my moth-er say, I heard my moth-er say,
2. Dark mid-night was my cry, dark mid-night was my cry,
3. Oh, when I come to die, oh, when I come to die,

I heard my moth-er say, "Give me Je - sus."
dark mid-night was my cry, give me Je - sus.
oh, when I come to die, give me Je - sus.

Refrain

Give me Je - sus, Give me Je - sus,

you may have all this world, give me Je - sus.

WORDS: Traditional
MUSIC: Traditional, arr. by Verolga Nix
Harm. © 1981 Abingdon Press, admin. by The Copyright Co.

The Glory of His Presence Medley
Oh, the Glory of His Presence 85

Then the cloud covered the tent of meeting,
and the glory of the LORD filled the tabernacle. (Exodus 40:34)

Oh, the glo - ry ___ of his pres - ence, ___ we your tem - ple ___ give him rev - erence. ___ Come and rise to his rest and be blest by our praise as we glo - ry in his em- brace: ___ as his pres - ence now fills this place. ___

WORDS: Steve Fry
MUSIC: Steve Fry

© 1983 BMG Songs/Birdwing Music (ASCAP), admin. by EMI CMG Publishing

86   The Glory of the Lord

And I looked, and lo! the glory of the LORD filled the temple of the LORD. (Ezekiel 44:4b)

When the glo-ry of the Lord fills this ho-ly tem-ple, he will lift us

high. And on an-gels' wings we'll rise to the pure and ho _ ly,

when his spir-it fills this place. When his glo - ry, when his

glo - ry, when his glo - ry fills this place. When his

glo - ry, when his glo - ry, when his glo - ry fills this place.

WORDS: Gloria Gaither, William Gaither, and Richard Smallwood
MUSIC: Gloria Gaither, William Gaither, and Richard Smallwood, arr. by Nolan Williams, Jr.

Anointing

The anointing that you received from him abides in you, and so … abide in him. (1 John 2:27)

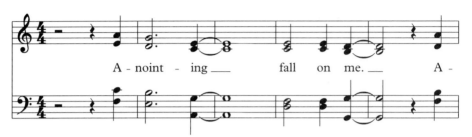

A - noint - ing ___ fall on me. ___ A -

noint - ing ___ fall on me. ___ Let the

pow - er of the Ho - ly Ghost fall on me. _

___ A - noint - ing fall on me.

WORDS: Donn C. Thomas
MUSIC: Donn C. Thomas, arr. by Evelyn Simpson-Curenton

End of **The Glory of His Presence Medley**

88 To Every Generation

LORD, you have been our dwelling place in all generations. (Psalm 90:1)

1. __ We re-mem-ber your mar - vel - ous works. __ From
2. A-mong your peo - ple you __ have dwelt, by your

grace to grace we've been led; _____ by your faith-ful
pres - ence we've been blessed. _ Young and old ex -

hand all things have been wrought _ for our good. Yes,
alt your name! Age to age _____ still the same, with

Refrain

we show faith and praise! _
grate - ful hearts we pro - claim! _

You have been a shel-

ter, Lord, to ev-ery gen-er-a - tion,

to ev-ery gen-er-a - tion. A sanc-tu - ar - y from _

__ the storm to ev-ery gen-er-a - tion,

to ev-ery gen-er-a - tion, Lord. _____

WORDS: Bill Batstone and Cynthia Wilson
MUSIC: Bill Batstone and Cynthia Wilson, arr. by William S. Moon

Koinonia

The commandment we have from him is this:
those who love God must love their brothers and sisters also. (1 John 4:21)

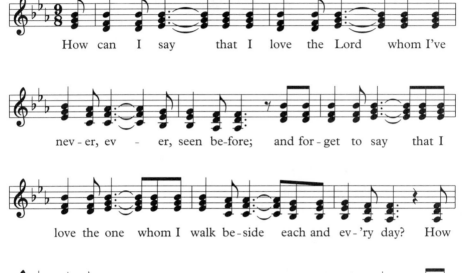

How can I say that I love the Lord whom I've

nev-er, ev - er, seen be-fore; and for-get to say that I

love the one whom I walk be-side each and ev-'ry day? How

can I look up - on your face and ig - nore God's love? You I

must em - brace! You're my broth-er; you're my

sis-ter; and I love you with the love of my

Lord. _____ Lord!

WORDS: Michael McKay
MUSIC: Michael McKay, arr. by William S. Moon

90 Dwell in Unity

How very good and pleasant it is when kindred live together in unity! (Psalm 133:1)

1. Be - hold how good and pleas-ant it is for
come share the fruit of the Spir - it, as

all of us to dwell in u - ni - ty, be -
God has giv - en you and me, with

hold how good and pleas-ant it is for
love joy peace and gen - tle - ness, we'll

all of us to dwell in u - ni - ty.
walk hand in hand in u - ni - ty.

WORDS: Pamela Jean Davis
MUSIC: Pamela Jean Davis, transcribed by Keith Hampton, arr. by Mark A. Miller

DWELL IN UNITY
Irregular

91 Who Is My Mother, Who Is My Brother

*"Here are my mother and my brothers! Whoever does the will of God
is my brother and sister and mother." (Mark 3:34b)*

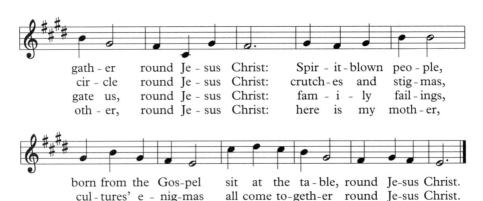

1. Who is my moth-er, who is my broth-er? all those who
2. Dif-ferent-ly a - bled, dif-ferent-ly la beled wid - en the
3. Love will re - late us — col - or or sta - tus can't se - gre -
4. Bound by one vi - sion, met for one mis-sion we claim each

gath - er round Je - sus Christ: Spir - it-blown peo - ple,
cir - cle round Je - sus Christ: crutch-es and stig - mas,
gate us, round Je - sus Christ: fam - i - ly fail - ings,
oth - er, round Je - sus Christ: here is my moth - er,

born from the Gos-pel sit at the ta - ble, round Je-sus Christ.
cul - tures' e - nig-mas all come to-geth-er round Je-sus Christ.
hu - man de - rail-ing — all are ac-cept-ed, round Je-sus Christ.
here is my broth-er, kin-dred in Spir-it, through Je-sus Christ.

WORDS: Shirley Erena Murray
MUSIC: Jack Schrader
© 1992 Hope Publishing Co.

KINDRED
54.54 D

92 There's No Me, There's No You

*So we, who are many, are one body in Christ,
and individually we are members one of another. (Romans 12:5)*

There's no me, there's no you with-out him. ____

__ There's no me, there's no you with-out him. ____

WORDS: Evelyn Reynolds, adapt. by Nolan Williams, Jr.
MUSIC: Evelyn Reynolds, arr. by Nolan Williams, Jr.
Adapt. and arr. © 2000 GIA Publications, Inc.

93 Make Us One

"The glory that you have given me I have given them,
so that they may be one, as we are one." (John 17:22)

Make us one, Lord, make us one; Ho-ly Spir-it, make us

one. Let your love flow so the world will know we are

Repeat ending / **Song ending**

one in you. Make us you.

WORDS: Carol Cymbala
MUSIC: Carol Cymbala

MAKE US ONE
Irregular

Step
(for Ushers)

94

I would rather be a doorkeeper in the house of my God
than live in the tents of wickedness. (Psalm 84:10b)

Group 1   Group 2   Group 1   Group 2   All

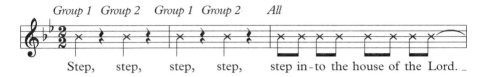

Step,   step,   step,   step,   step in-to the house of the Lord. _

Group 1   Group 2   Group 1   Group 2

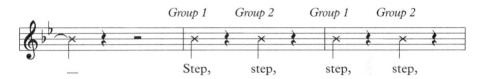

Step,   step,   step,   step,

All   *Fine*

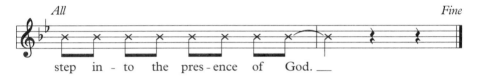

step   in - to   the   pres - ence   of   God. __

1. We're keep-ers   of   the   door,   the
2. The Lord is   sun   and shield,   our
3. Come wea - ry   soul, find   rest.   Rise

guar-dians   of God's house;   we   wait to   greet   you   at   the
God who reigns on   high;   the   Ho - ly   Pres - ence   in   this
faint - ing   heart, be   strong.   For   Je - sus Christ gives awe-some

D.C. al Fine

gate   and   ush-er you in   to   sing God's   praise.
place.   We   ush-er you in   to   sing God's   praise.
grace.   We   ush-er you in   to   sing God's   praise.

WORDS: Gennifer Benjamin Brooks
MUSIC: Marilyn E. Thornton

95 Rule of Life

Show me your faith apart from your works,
and I by my works will show you my faith. (James 2:18b)

Do all the good you can, ___ by all the means you can, __

__ in all the ways you can ___ in all the plac-es you can, __

__ at all the times you can ___ to all the peo-ple you can, __

__ as long as ev - er ___ you can. ___

WORDS: An 18th century aphorism, attr. to John Wesley
MUSIC: Edward Bonnemere, arr. by Cynthia Wilson

© 1979 Amity Music

96 Affirmation

Jesus said to him, "No one who puts a hand to the plow and looks back
is fit for the kingdom of God." (Luke 9:62)

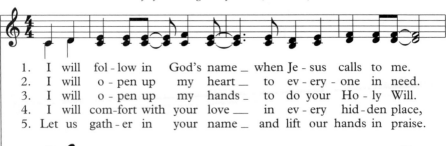

1. I will fol - low in God's name _ when Je - sus calls to me.
2. I will o - pen up my heart _ to ev - ery - one in need.
3. I will o - pen up my hands _ to do your Ho - ly Will.
4. I will com-fort with your love _ in ev - ery hid - den place,
5. Let us gath - er in your name _ and lift our hands in praise.

WORDS: Marilyn E. Thornton
MUSIC: Marilyn E. Thornton

KELVINGROVE
13 13 7 7 13

© 2007 Abingdon Press, admin. by The Copyright Co.

I will trust you just the same _ wher-ev - er I may
I will move to do my part __ for shac-kles to be
I will give up ev - ery plan, _ your pur-pose to ful -
with your Spir - it from a - bove _ so they may know your
You will break off ev - ery chain _ and val - leys you will

be. I will seek your will to do; ___ I will
freed. Ev - ery ac - tion, ev - ery word, _ ev - ery
fill. For the peo - ple - far and near, _ I will
grace. Man - y blind - ed souls will see, ___ and the
raise. I will sing from moun-tains high. _ I will

tell the gos - pel news. _ I will ev - er hope in you __
part of me will serve. _ I will let your voice be heard _
show them that we care; _ I will be your pres - ence there _
truth will set them free. _ May your Spir - it shine in me __
fol - low till I die. _ With your peo - ple, I'll a - bide _

2

_ so you may use me.
_ so you may use me.
_ so you can use me.
_ so you may use me.
_ so you may use me.

2

97 How Like a Gentle Spirit

By the tender mercy of our God the dawn from on high will break upon us...
to guide our feet into the way of peace. (Luke 1:78-79)

1. How like a gen - tle spir - it deep with - in God
2. Let God be God wher - ev - er life may be, let
3. God like a moth - er ea - gle hov - ers near on
4. When in our vain pre - ten - tions we con - spire to

reigns our fer - vent pas - sions day by day, and
ev - ery tongue bear wit - ness to the call; all
might - y wings of pow - er man - i - fest; God
shape God's im - age as we see our own, hark

gives us strength to chal - lenge and to win de -
hu - man - kind is one by God's de - cree; let
like a gen - tle shep - herd stills our fear, and
to the voice a - bove our base de - sire; God

spite the per - ils of our cho - sen way.
God be God, let God be God for all.
com - forts us a - gainst a peace - ful breast.
is the sculp - tor, we the bro - ken stone.

WORDS: C. Eric Lincoln
MUSIC: Mark A. Miller
Words © 1989 The United Methodist Publishing House; music © 2005 Mark A. Miller

BALTIMORE
10.10.10.10

98 He Who Began a Good Work in You

I am confident of this, that the one who began a good work among you
will bring it to completion by the day of Jesus Christ. (Philippians 1:6)

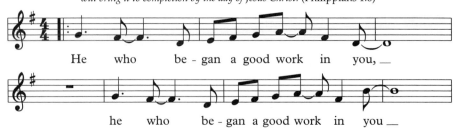

He who be - gan a good work in you, —

he who be - gan a good work in you —

WORDS: Jon Mohr
MUSIC: Jon Mohr
© 1987 Jonathan Mark Music and Birdwing Music

A GOOD WORK
Irregular

We All Are One in Mission 99

Now there are varieties of gifts, but the same Spirit; and there are varieties of services, but the same Lord. (1 Corinthians 12:4-5)

1. We all are one in mis - sion, we all are one in call, ___
2. We all are called for ser - vice, to wit-ness in God's name. _
3. Now let us be u - nit - ed, and let our song be heard. _

— our var - ied gifts u - nit - ed by
— Our min - is - tries are dif - ferent; our
— Now let us be a ves - sel for

Christ, the Lord of all. ___ A sin - gle great com-mis-
pur - pose is the same. _ To touch the lives of oth-
God's re - deem - ing word. _ We all are one in mis-

sion com-pels us from a - bove ___ to plan and work to-geth-
ers by God's sur-pris-ing grace, _ so ev - ery folk and na -
sion, we all are one in call, ___ our var - ied gifts u - ni -

er that all may know Christ's love. ___
tion may feel God's warm em - brace. _
ed by Christ, the Lord of all. ___

WORDS: Rusty Edwards
MUSIC: Marilyn E. Thornton, arr. by Mark A. Miller

Words © 1986 Hope Publishing Co.; music © 2007 Abingdon Press, admin. by The Copyright Co.

100 Grace Alone

For by grace you have been saved through faith,
and this is not your own doing; it is the gift of God. (Ephesians 2:8)

1. Ev - ery prom - ise we can make, ev - ery prayer and
2. Ev - ery soul we long to reach, ev - ery heart we

step of faith, ev - ery dif - ference we will make
hope to teach, ev - ery - where we share his peace

is on - ly by his grace. Ev - ery moun - tain
is on - ly by his grace. Ev - ery lov - ing

we will climb, ev - ery ray of hope we shine,
word we say, ev - ery tear we wipe a - way,

ev - ery bless - ing left be - hind ⎫
ev - ery sor - row turned to praise ⎬ is on - ly by his

Refrain

grace. Grace a - lone which God sup-plies, strength un-

known he will pro-vide. Christ in us our Cor-ner-

Repeat ending

stone; we will go forth in grace a - lone.

WORDS: Scott Wesley Brown and Jeff Nelson
MUSIC: Scott Wesley Brown and Jeff Nelson
GRACE ALONE
Irregular with Refrain

Song ending

lone.

Optional choral ending
(mel. in lowest notes) **f**

lone. Grace a - lone which God sup-plies, strength un-

known he will pro-vide. Christ in us our Cor-ner-

unis.

stone; we will go forth in grace a - lone. Grace a-

lone which God sup-plies, strength un-known he will pro-

unis. **mp**

vide. Christ in us our Cor-ner-stone; we will go

rit. *slower* **mp**

forth in grace a - lone. We will go forth

molto rit.

in grace a - lone.

101 I Give All to You

She out of her poverty has put in all she had to live on. (Luke 21:4b)

1. I give all my ser-vice to you, I give
2. I give all my prob-lems to you, I give
3. I give all my fam-ily to you, I give
4. I give all my fu-ture to you, I give
5. I give all my wor-ship to you, I give

all my ser-vice to you; no mat-ter the cost or
all my prob-lems to you; no mat-ter the cost or
all my fam-ily to you; no mat-ter the cost or
all my fu-ture to you; no mat-ter the cost or
all my wor-ship to you; no mat-ter the cost or

what oth-ers do, I give all my ser-vice to you.
what oth-ers do, I give all my prob-lems to you.
what oth-ers do, I give all my fam-ily to you.
what oth-ers do, I give all my fu-ture to you.
what oth-ers do, I give all my wor-ship to you.

WORDS: Larnelle Harris
MUSIC: Larnelle Harris, arr. by William S. Moon

World Without Walls

What is the house that you would build for me, and what is my resting place? (Isaiah 66:1b)

1. Place my feet on the land where no bar - ri - ers
2. With God's grace from a - bove fill each heart with such
3. Quick - ly sound through the din o - ver col - or of
4. Help the young work with old, and the rich share their
5. Ev - ery - one on this earth is our neigh - bor by

stand, and its peo - ple have sense
love that we cease from our fights
skin, through the pris - m seems white,
gold; make our ig - no - rance flee,
birth, and our Lord has de - creed

to re - ject ev - ery fence till each ob - sta - cle
while we prize what u - nites and we teach in our
it's all col - ors of light that are blend - ed by
and its slaves be set free till we help those who
that we hear and we heed as hu - man - i - ty

falls in a world with - out walls.
halls of a world with - out walls.
all in a world with - out walls.
fall in a world with - out walls.
calls for a world with - out walls.

WORDS: David A. Robb and Amanda Husberg
MUSIC: Newlove Annan

This music comes in the musical (rhythmic) style called the
"Hi Life." Hi Life Music or rhythm, was created in the
western part of Africa. It is basically a fusion of Caribbean,
West and Central African indigenous rhythms, such as
Calypso, Samba, Kwasa, and Kpanlogo. It is a danceable
rhythm.

103   There's a Spirit of Love in This Place

Above all, clothe yourselves with love,
which binds everything together in perfect harmony. (Colossians 3:14)

1. There's a   spir - it of love   in this place,   there's a
(2. There's the)   pres - ence of peace   in this room,   there's the

spir - it   of love   in this place.   You can't
pres - ence of peace   in this room.   In God's

see it, but it's there, just   as pre-cious as the   air. There's a
ten-der-ness is found peace that pass - es   hu-man bounds. There's the

spir - it   of love   in this place.   2. There's the
pres - ence of peace   in this

Refrain
room.   O al - le - lu - ia,   sing al - le - lu - ia!   We

bless your ho - ly   name.   O al - le - lu - ia,   sing al - le -

lu - ia!   There's a   spir - it of love   in this place.

WORDS: Mark A. Miller   MEDEMA
MUSIC: Mark A. Miller   Irregular

Ain't Gonna Let Nobody
Turn Me 'Round*

104

*I press on toward the goal for the prize
of the heavenly call of God in Christ Jesus.* (Philippians 3:14)

Strutting tempo

Ain't gon-na let no-**bod-y turn me 'round, turn me 'round, turn me 'round. Ain't gon-na let no - bod - y turn me 'round, I'm gon - na keep on a - walk - in', keep on a - talk - in', march-in' on to free-dom land. _

Alternate words: 'til the day I die. __

**Change this word only for each new verse.*

2. segregation
3. persecution
4. hatred
5. jail house
6. police dogs
7. billy club (night stick)
8. fire hose
9. tear gas

WORDS: African American spiritual
MUSIC: African American spiritual, arr. by Lavinia L. T. Odejimi
Arr. © 2007 Abingdon Press, admin. by The Copyright Co.

*This song, like many others, was adapted from a historical
spiritual to meet the needs of the Civil Rights Movement.

Original words:

Don't you let nobody turn you 'round, turn you 'round, turn you 'round,
Don't you let nobody turn you 'round, you gotta keep on a-walkin',
Keep on a-talkin', marchin' on to Canaan land.

105 Woke Up This Morning

But I will sing of your might;
I will sing aloud of your steadfast love in the morning. (Psalm 59:16a)

1. Woke up this morn-ing with my mind stayed on Je - sus.
2. Woke up this morn-ing with my mind stayed on free-dom.
3. Walk - in' and talk - in' with my mind stayed on free-dom.
4. Can't hate your neigh-bor with your mind stayed on free-dom.

Woke up this morn-ing with my mind stayed on Je - sus.
Woke up this morn-ing with my mind stayed on free-dom.
Walk - in' and talk - in' with my mind stayed on free-dom.
Can't hate your neigh-bor with your mind stayed on free-dom.

Woke up this morn-ing with my mind
Woke up this morn-ing with my mind
Walk - in' and talk - in' with my mind
Can't hate your neigh-bor with your mind

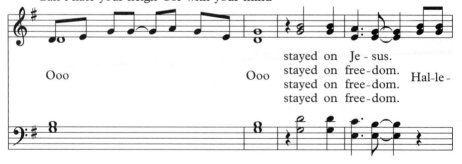

Ooo Ooo

stayed on Je - sus.
stayed on free-dom.
stayed on free-dom.
stayed on free-dom.

Hal-le -

WORDS: African American spiritual
MUSIC: African American spiritual, arr. by Marilyn E. Thornton
Arr. © 2007 Abingdon Press, admin. by The Copyright Co.

WOKE UP THIS MORNING
Irregular

lu,   hal-le - lu,   hal-le - lu   -   jah!

Hal-le - lu,   *hal-le - lu, hal-le - lu*   -   *jah!*

We Shall Overcome   106

*Who is it that conquers the world
but the one who believes that Jesus is the Son of God?* (1 John 5:5)

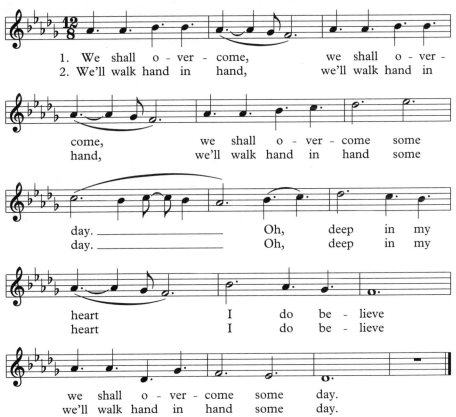

1. We shall o - ver - come,   we shall o - ver -
2. We'll walk hand in hand,   we'll walk hand in

come,   we shall o - ver - come some
hand,   we'll walk hand in hand some

day. _____ Oh, deep in my
day. _____ Oh, deep in my

heart   I do be - lieve
heart   I do be - lieve

we shall o - ver - come some day.
we'll walk hand in hand some day.

*Inspired by African American Gospel Singing, members of the Food & Tobacco Workers Union, Charleston, South Carolina,
and the southern Civil Rights Movement. Royalties derived from this composition are being contributed to the We Shall
Overcome Fund and The Freedom Movement under the Trusteeship of the writers.*

WORDS: Trad., adapt. by Zilphia Horton, Frank Hamilton, Guy Carawan, and Pete Seeger   MARTIN
MUSIC: Trad., adapt. by Zilphia Horton, Frank Hamilton, Guy Carawan, and Pete Seeger;   Irregular
       arr. by Monya Davis Logan

107 Freedom Afterwhile

Neither shall they learn war anymore...and no one shall make them afraid. (Micah 4:3b, 4b)

1. Free-dom, free-dom, free-dom af - ter - while.
2. Peace, peace, peace af - ter - while.
3. Shout, shout, shout af - ter - while.
4. Joy, joy, joy af - ter - while.

Fine

Free-dom, free-dom, free-dom af - ter - while.
Peace, peace, peace af - ter - while.
Shout, shout, shout af - ter - while.
Joy, joy, joy af - ter - while.

1. One day this war will be o - ver, we'll
2. This world is full of sor - row, crying

lay our ar - mor down. Walk on up the
on ev - er - y hand. God's gon - na wipe

D.C.

King's high - way, and get our star - ry crown.
all tears a - way, and lead us to the prom-ised land.

WORDS: Michael L. Charles
MUSIC: Michael L. Charles
© 1975 Michael L. Charles

Spiritual Medley for Pentecost 108

But those who wait on the LORD shall renew their strength, they shall mount up with wings like eagles, they shall run and not be weary, they shall walk and not faint. (Isaiah 40:31)

WORDS: Trad. African American
MUSIC: Trad. African American, arr. by Cynthia Wilson

© 2007 Cynthia Wilson

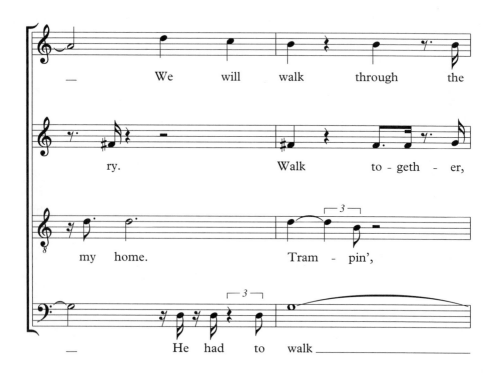

walk through the val - ley in peace. _

Walk to-geth - er, chil - dren,

Tram - pin', tram - pin',

walk _____ it by him -

_____ When we

don't you get wea - ry. When we

tryin' to make heab - 'n my home. When we

self. When we

all _____ get to heav - en, __ what a

day of re - joic - ing that will be. _____ When we __

__ all _____ see Je - sus we'll sing and

shout the vic - to - ry. __ When we

Freedom Medley
O Freedom
109

The small and the great are there, and the slaves are free from their masters. (Job 3:19)

O free-dom, O free-dom,

O free-dom o - ver me _____ and be -

fore I'll be a slave, _ I'll be bur-ied in my grave _

__ and go home to my Lord _ and be free. _

WORDS: African American spiritual
MUSIC: African American spiritual, arr. by William S. Moon
Arr. © 2007 Abingdon Press, admin. by The Copyright Co.

O FREEDOM
Irregular with Refrain

110 Freedom Is Coming

So if the Son makes you free, you will be free indeed. (John 8:36)

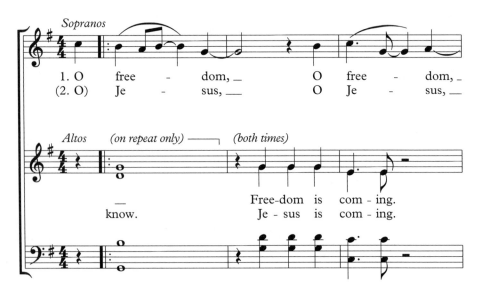

1. O free - dom, — O free - dom, —
(2. O) Je - sus, — O Je - sus, —

Altos *(on repeat only)* *(both times)*

— Free-dom is com - ing.
know. Je - sus is com - ing.

— O free - dom, —
— O Je - sus, —

Free-dom is com - ing. Free-dom is com - ing, O
Je - sus is com - ing. Je - sus is com - ing, O

WORDS: Trad. South African
MUSIC: Trad. South African
© 1964 Utryck, admin. by Walton Music Group

FREEDOM IS COMING
Irregular

End of **Freedom Medley**

111

We Are Singing
(Siyahamba/Caminando)

But now in the Lord, you are light. Live as children of light. (Ephesians 5:8b)

(English) We are sing - ing* in the
(Zulu**) Si - ya - hamb' e - ku - kha -
(Spanish) Ca - mi - nan - do en la

light of God, we are sing-ing in the light of God. _
nyen' kwen - khos', si - ya - hamb' e - ku - kha-nyen' kwen - khos. _
luz de Dios, ca - mi - nan - do en la luz de Dios. _

1.

2.
of God _
kwen - khos' _
de Dios _

We are sing - ing in the light of, the
Si - ya - hamb e - ku - kha-nyen' kwen kha -
Ca - mi - nan - do en la luz de, la

of God _
kwen - khos' _
de Dios _

*walking, ringing, marching, dancing, praying, etc.

WORDS: South Africa (20th cent.)
MUSIC: South Africa (20th cent.)

SIYAHAMBA
Irregular

112   We Are Real People

"He has sent me to proclaim release to the captives…to let the oppressed go free." (Luke 4:18b)

1. I am a South Af - ri - can
2. Come on peo - ple be named
3. Bo - tha and Tu - tu _____ talked

— I am black.
— a - mong us
the oth - er night.

I want peace in my
hu - man - i - ty is
A - bout the pain and

coun - try
bound up
suf - fer - ing and the

that's a fact.
in our cause.
peo - ple's plight.

I've been
If you
He said

told what to do and I've been told
say you be - lieve in God, in God,
I'm a Bish - op and I don't have a vote in my

what to say.
God at all.
coun - try.

I want my peo - ple and theirs to throw
— Cry a - loud and spare not less
— Give us back our birth - right.

Last time to Coda ⊕   *Refrain*

ha - tred a - way.
all of us fall.
We will be free!

We don't want our

shack - les pol - ished. We want them re - moved.

WORDS: Donn Thomas
MUSIC: Donn Thomas

113 Lift Every Voice and Sing

Be filled with the Spirit, as you sing psalms and hymns
and spiritual songs…giving thanks to God. (Ephesians 5:18b-20a)

1. Lift ev-ery voice and sing, till earth and heav - en ring,
2. Ston-y the road we trod, bit - ter the chas -tening rod,
3. God of our wea - ry years, God of our si - lent tears,

ring with the har - mo - nies of lib - er - ty;
felt in the days when hope un - born had died;
thou who hast brought us thus far on the way;

let our re - joic - ing rise, high as the lis - tening skies,
yet with a stead - y beat, have not our wea - ry feet,
thou who hast by thy might, led us in - to the light,

let it re - sound loud as the roll - ing sea.
come to the place for which our fa - thers sighed?
keep us for - ev - er in the path, we pray.

WORDS: James Weldon Johnson
MUSIC: J. Rosamond Johnson

LIFT EVERY VOICE
Irregular

© 1921 Edward B. Marks Music Co.

Sing a song full of the faith that the dark past has taught us,
We have come o - ver a way that with tears has been wa - tered,
Lest our feet stray from the plac - es, our God, where we meet thee,

sing a song full of the hope that the pres - ent has brought
we have come, tread - ing our path thro' the blood of the slaugh -
lest our hearts, drunk with the wine of the world, we for - get

us; fac - ing the ris - ing sun of our new day be -
tered, out from the gloom - y past, till now we stand at
thee; shad-owed be - neath thy hand, may we for - ev - er

gun, let us march on till vic - to - ry is won.
last where the white gleam of our bright star is cast.
stand, true to our God, true to our na - tive land.

114 There Is a Balm

Is there no balm in Gilead? Is there no physician there? (Jeremiah 8:22*a*)

There is a balm in Gil-e-ad, to make the wound-ed
whole; _____ there is a balm in Gil-e-ad, to
heal the sin - sick soul.

Fine

1. Some-times I feel dis-
2. If you can't preach like

cour-aged, and think my work's in vain, but then the Ho-ly
Pe - ter, if you can't pray like Paul, just tell the love of

WORDS: African American spiritual
MUSIC: African American spiritual, arr. by William S. Moon
Arr. © 2007 Abingdon Press, admin. by The Copyright Co.

BALM IN GILEAD
Irregular

D.S. al Fine

Spir - it re - vives my soul a - gain. _____ There is a
Je - sus, and say he died for all. _____

I Will Restore 115

For I will restore health to you, and your wounds I will heal. (Jeremiah 30:17a)

What was lost in bat-tle, what was tak-en un-law-ful, where the

en - e - my has plant - ed his seed, and where

health is ail - ing and your strength is fail - ing I will re-

store to you all of this and more. I will re - store, I will re-

store, I will re-store to you all of this and more. I will re-

store, I will re - store, I will re-store to you all of this and

more. I will re-store to you all of this and more.

WORDS: Richard Johnson
MUSIC: Richard Johnson, arr. by William S. Moon

116 Give Me a Clean Heart

Create in me a clean heart, O God, and put a new and right spirit within me. (Psalm 51:10)

Refrain

Give me a clean heart so I may serve thee, Lord, fix my

heart so that I may be used by thee. For I'm not

wor - thy of all these bless - ings. Give me a

clean heart ___ and I'll fol-low thee. ___

1. I'm not
(2. _ Some-)

1. ask - ing for the rich - es of the land. ___ I'm not
2. times I'm up and some-times I am down. ___ Some-times

1. ask - ing for high men to know my name. ___ Please
2. I am al - most lev - el to the ground. ___ Please

1. give me, Lord, a clean heart, that I may fol-low thee. Give me a
2. give me, Lord, a clean heart, that I may fol-low thee. Give me a

1. clean heart, a clean heart and I will fol-low thee. ___
2. clean heart, a clean heart and I will fol-low thee. ___

WORDS: Margaret Pleasant Douroux
MUSIC: Margaret Pleasant Douroux, arr. by Albert Dennis Tessier

DOUROUX
Irregular

2. Some -

Glory, Glory, Hallelujah! 117

"I relieved your shoulder of the burden; your hands were freed from the basket." (Psalm 81:6)

1. Glo - ry, glo - ry, _____ hal - le - lu - jah! _____
2. I feel bet - ter, _____ so much bet - ter _____
3. Feel like shout - in' _____ "Hal - le - lu - jah!" _____
4. Friends don't treat me _____ like they used to _____
5. I'm goin' home to _____ live with Je - sus _____

_ since I laid my _____ bur - dens down. -
_ since I laid my _____ bur - dens down. -
_ since I laid my _____ bur - dens down. -
_ since I laid my _____ bur - dens down. -
_ since I laid my _____ bur - dens down. -

Glo - ry, glo - ry, _____ hal - le - lu - jah! _____
I feel bet - ter, _____ so much bet - ter _____
Feel like shout - in' _____ "Hal - le - lu - jah!" _____
Friends don't treat me _____ like they used to _____
I'm goin' home to _____ live with Je - sus _____

_ since I laid my _____ bur-dens down. _
_ since I laid my _____ bur-dens down. _
_ since I laid my _____ bur-dens down. _
_ since I laid my _____ bur-dens down. _
_ since I laid my _____ bur-dens down. _

WORDS: Trad.
MUSIC: Trad., arr. by Mark A. Miller
Arr. © 2007 Abingdon Press, admin. by The Copyright Co.

GLORY
15 15

118 — Come On in My Room

Then he put them all outside, and took the child's father and mother and those who were with him, and went in where the child was. (Mark 5:40)

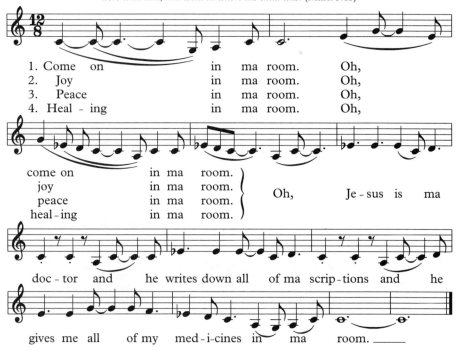

1. Come on in ma room. Oh,
2. Joy in ma room. Oh,
3. Peace in ma room. Oh,
4. Heal - ing in ma room. Oh,

come on in ma room.
joy in ma room.
peace in ma room.
heal - ing in ma room.

Oh, Je - sus is ma

doc - tor and he writes down all of ma scrip - tions and he

gives me all of my med - i - cines in ma room. ____

WORDS: African American traditional
MUSIC: African American traditional, arr. by Cecilia L. Clemons
Arr. © 2007 Cecilia L. Clemons

119 — Heal Me

They laid the sick in the marketplaces, and begged him that they might touch even the fringe of his cloak; and all who touched it were healed. (Mark 6:56b)

Heal me, ____ heal me, ____ I need a brand new

touch from you, my Lord; ____ heal me, ____ heal me, _

__ let the full - ness of your life now be re - stored. ____

WORDS: Terry MacAlmon
MUSIC: Terry MacAlmon
© 2001 TMMI Music (ASCAP), admin. by Music Services

Father, I Stretch My Hands to Thee   120

I stretch out my hands to you; my soul thirsts for you like a parched land. (Psalm 143:6)

1. Fa - ther, I stretch my hands to thee, no oth -
2. What did thine on - ly Son en - dure, be - fore
3. Sure - ly thou canst not let me die, O speak
4. Au - thor of faith! to thee I lift my wear -

er help I know; if thou with - draw thy - self
I drew my breath! What pain, what la - bor to
and I shall live; and here I will un - wear -
y, long - ing eyes; O let me now re - ceive

from me, Ah! whith - er shall I go?
se - cure my soul from end - less death!
ied lie, till thou thy Spir - it give.
that gift! My soul with - out it dies.

WORDS: Charles Wesley   MARTYRDOM
MUSIC: Hugh Wilson, lined by J. Jefferson Cleveland and Verolga Nix   CM
Arr. © 1979 J. Jefferson Cleveland/Verolga Nix

Higher, Higher   121

*For your steadfast love is higher than the heavens,
and your faithfulness reaches to the clouds.* (Psalm 108:4)

1. High-er, high-er,   high-er, high-er, high-er, high-er,
2. Low-er, low-er,   low-er, low-er, low-er, low-er,
3. Su-per, su-per,   su-per, su-per, su-per, su-per,

high-er, high-er.   Lift Je - sus high-er!
low-er, low-er.   Stomp the dev - il low-er!
su-per, su-per.   Su - per-nat - u-ral pow-er!

WORDS: Anonymous
MUSIC: Anonymous, arr. by Nolan Williams, Jr.
Arr. © 2000 GIA Publications, Inc.

122   Come and Go with Me

"Come, let us go up to the mountain of the LORD, to the house of the God of Jacob;
that he may teach us his ways and that we may walk in his paths." (Micah 4:2)

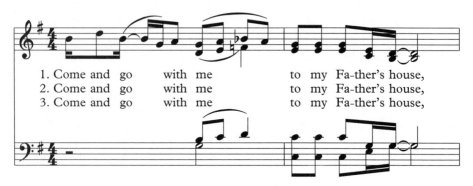

1. Come and go with me to my Fa-ther's house,
2. Come and go with me to my Fa-ther's house,
3. Come and go with me to my Fa-ther's house,

to my Fa-ther's house to my Fa-ther's house.
to my Fa-ther's house to my Fa-ther's house.
to my Fa-ther's house to my Fa-ther's house.

Come and go with me to my Fa-ther's house there is
Come and go with me to my Fa-ther's house there is
Come and go with me to my Fa-ther's house there is

WORDS: Trad. African American
MUSIC: Trad. African American, arr. by Marilyn E. Thornton
Arr. © 2007 Abingdon Press, admin. by The Copyright Co.

COME AND GO WITH ME
10 10 10 5

joy,   joy,   joy.
peace,   peace,   peace.
love,   love,   love.

Victory Is Mine   123

But thanks be to God, who gives us the victory through our Lord Jesus Christ. (1 Corinthians 15:57)

1. Vic - to - ry   is mine.   Vic - to - ry   is mine.
2. Joy   is mine.   Joy   is mine.
3. Hap - pi - ness   is mine.   Hap - pi - ness   is mine.

Vic - to - ry   to-day is   mine. _   I told Sa - tan
Joy   to-day is   mine. _   I told Sa - tan
Hap-pi - ness   to-day is   mine. _   I told Sa - tan

get thee be-hind.   Vic - to - ry   to-day is   mine. _
get thee be-hind.   Joy   to-day is   mine. _
get thee be-hind.   Hap-pi - ness   to-day is   mine. _

WORDS: Dorothy Norwood and Alvin Darling
MUSIC: Dorothy Norwood and Alvin Darling

VICTORY
5 5 7 8 7

124   I Thank You, Jesus

He prostrated himself at Jesus' feet and thanked him. And he was a Samaritan. (Luke 17:16)

WORDS: Kenneth Morris
MUSIC: Kenneth Morris, arr. by Joseph Joubert

125 The Lord Is Blessing Me Right Now

Blessed be the God and Father of our Lord Jesus Christ,
who has blessed us in Christ with every spiritual blessing. (Ephesians 1:3)

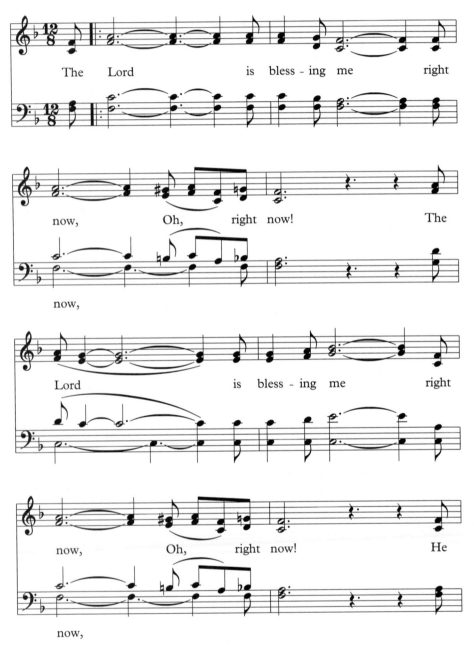

The Lord is bless - ing me right
now, Oh, right now! The

Lord is bless - ing me right
now, Oh, right now! He

now,

WORDS: Trad. Gospel
MUSIC: Trad. Gospel, arr. by Nolan Williams, Jr.

woke me up this morn - ing, and

start - ed me on my way; the

Lord is bless - ing me right

1
now!

2
The now! _____

126 I Remember

Remember me, O LORD, when you show favor to your people; …
that I may glory in your heritage. (Psalm 106:4-5)

I remember as my mind rolls back,
I recall, I recollect
the symptoms of manmade emblems,
bound by fallacies and insecurities.
Instead of the bondage of realities
presented, represented by "G" "O" "D."
I was flying, I was trying,
I was lying, I was dying.

Crying out for multiple infusions,
needing someone to touch and heal my wounds.
I remember bold words spoke
told Revelation, the patience, the love that was shown.
Like a train full speed on a straight forward track,
I got on his promises to never turn back.
From this, yes, I know this day I recollect
and like the words of Moses:

Chorus
I remember what God did for me.
I remember how God blessed me.
I remember all the great things God's done.
I remember, God gave us his only Son.
How God brought me out, I remember.
How God showed me the route, I remember.
How God forgave my sins, I remember.
How I gave my life to him, I remember.

Now on this track, now let's flash back
and look at all the times where you almost fell flat.
Almost didn't make it through these troubles you was facing,
you question in your mind, how I'm gonna make it.
I remember, I know you had some very hard times,
rejected but you never gave up, you always tried.
Now God made everything come through,
now remember all the things that God did for you.

Chorus

WORDS: Frederick Burchell and Craig Watkins
MUSIC: Frederick Burchell and Kyle Lovett
© 2006 B4 Entertainment

If he'll do it once, he'll do it again,
so don't forget about all the great things he did.
God split the Red Sea, made Israel free,
Jesus made the blind see, made the lame move his feet.
Every morning his mercies are brand new,
so mark it permanently just like a tattoo in your mind.
Jesus, he died on the cross,
he rose from the dead, so you don't have to be lost.

I remember God saved Noah from the flood
and Jesus loves you with so much love.
I remember, and God invites everyone to come.
God created the moon and the sun,
and God saved Daniel from the lion's den,
and God gave Paul his sight again.
I remember, it's as simple as this,
God brought us out and blessed us, so don't forget this.

   Chorus

126   I Remember

Remember me, O LORD, when you show favor to your people; …
that I may glory in your heritage. (Psalm 106:4-5)

Chorus

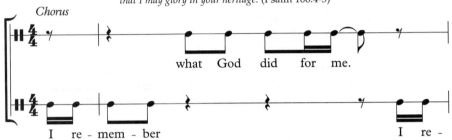

what God did for me.

I re - mem - ber   I re -

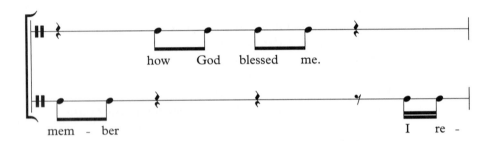

how God blessed me.

mem - ber   I re -

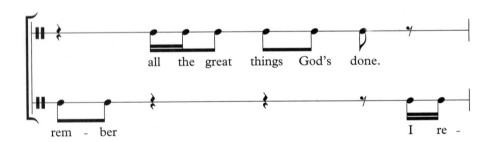

all the great things God's done.

rem - ber   I re -

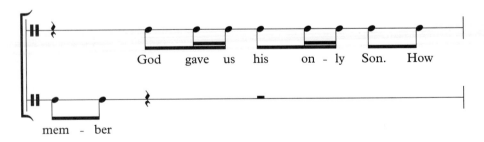

God gave us his on - ly Son. How

mem - ber

WORDS: Frederick Burchell and Craig Watkins
MUSIC: Frederick Burchell and Kyle Lovett

© 2006 B4 Entertainment

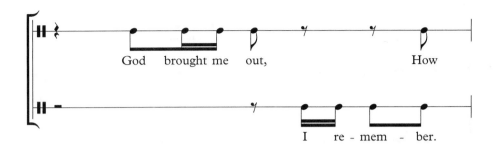

God brought me out, How

I re - mem - ber.

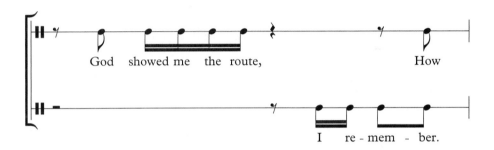

God showed me the route, How

I re - mem - ber.

God for - gave my sins, How

I re - mem - ber.

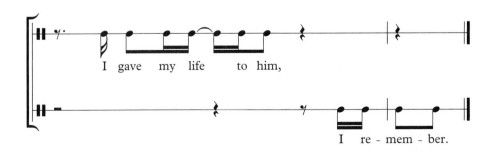

I gave my life to him,

I re - mem - ber.

127 Give Thanks

By him therefore let us offer the sacrifice of praise to God continually, that is,
the fruit of our lips giving thanks to his name. (Hebrews 13:15 KJV)

Give thanks with a grate-ful heart, give thanks to the

Ho-ly One, give thanks be-cause he's giv-en Je-sus

Christ, his Son. Give thanks with a grate-ful heart, give

thanks to the Ho-ly One, give thanks be-cause he's

giv-en Je-sus Christ, his Son. And now let the

weak say, "I am strong"; let the poor say, "I am rich be-cause of

what the Lord has done for us." And now let the

weak say, "I am strong"; let the poor say, "I am rich be-cause of

what the Lord has done for us." Give us." Give thanks. ___

___ Give thanks. ___ Give thanks. ___ Give thanks. ___ thanks.

WORDS: Henry Smith
MUSIC: Henry Smith, arr. by Oscar Dismuke

GIVE THANKS
Irregular

Your Grace and Mercy

128

*But by the grace of God I am what I am,
and his grace toward me has not been in vain.* (1 Corinthians 15:10)

Your grace and mer - cy brought me through, I'm liv-ing this

mo - ment be-cause of you; I want to thank you, and praise you

Last time to Coda ⊕   *D.S.*

too: your grace and mer - cy brought me through. Your grace and

⊕ CODA   *Repeat as desired.*

mer - cy your grace and mer - cy brought me through.

WORDS: Franklin D. Williams
MUSIC: Franklin D. Williams

129   Watch Night

"Keep awake therefore, for you do not know on what day your Lord is coming." (Matthew 24:42)

1. From a sea - son of light to the
2. Time for birth, life, and death filled with
3. Ho - ly ci - ty from heaven, God has

dawn of new day; from the dark-ness of night, heaven and
sad-ness and joy; God has given us new breath, grace that
built it on earth; that all peo - ple may live joined with

earth passed a - way; give us new-ness of life, just - tice,
we may em - ploy in the toils of our days faith that
Christ in new birth. God has made all things new, ho - ly

peace with - out strife so the year that be-gins may be love.
nev - er will sway so the year that a - waits may be joy.
righ-teous and true, so the year that un-folds may be peace.

WORDS: Gennifer Benjamin Brooks
MUSIC: Marilyn E. Thornton

130   The Right Hand of God

The right hand of the LORD is exalted; the right hand of the LORD does valiantly. (Psalm 118:16)

1. The right hand of God is writ - ing in our
2. The right hand of God is point-ing in our
3. The right hand of God is strik-ing in our
4. The right hand of God is heal-ing in our
5. The right hand of God is plant-ing in our

WORDS: Patrick Prescod
MUSIC: Noel Dexter

land, writ - ing with pow - er and with
land, point - ing the way we must
land, strik - ing out at en - vy, hate, and
land, heal - ing bro - ken bod - ies, minds, and
land, plant - ing seeds of free - dom, hope, and

love, _____ our con - flicts and our
go. _____ So cloud - ed is the
greed. _____ Our self - ish - ness and
souls. _____ So won-drous is its
love. _____ In these Ca - rib - bean

fears, our tri-umphs and our tears are re -
way, so eas - i - ly we stray, but we're
lust, our pride and deeds un - just, are de -
touch with love that means so much, when we're
lands, let his peo - ple all join hands and be

cord - ed by the right hand of God.
guid - ed by the right hand of God.
stroyed by the right hand of God.
healed by the right hand of God.
one with the right hand of God.

131 When We All Get to Heaven

We have a building from God, a house not made with hands,
eternal in the heavens. (2 Corinthians 5:1b)

1. Sing the won-drous love of Je - sus; sing his mer - cy
2. While we walk the pil - grim path-way, clouds will o - ver -
3. Let us then be true and faith - ful, trust - ing, serv - ing
4. On - ward to the prize be - fore us! Soon his beau - ty

and his grace. In the man - sions bright and bless - ed
spread the sky; but when trav - eling days are o - ver,
ev - ery day; just one glimpse of him in glo - ry
we'll be - hold; soon the pearl - y gates will o - pen;

Refrain

he'll pre - pare for us a place.
not a shad-ow, not a sigh.
will the toils of life re - pay. When we all get to
we shall tread the streets of gold.

heav - en, what a day of re-joic-ing that will be! When we

all see Je - sus, we'll sing and shout the vic-to - ry!

WORDS: Eliza Edmunds Hewitt HEAVEN
MUSIC: Emily Divine Wilson, arr. by Regina Hoosier, transcribed by Marilyn E. Thornton 87.87 with Refrain
Arr. © 2007 Regina Hoosier (ASCAP)

132 The Jesus in Me

Let mutual love continue. (Hebrews 13:1)

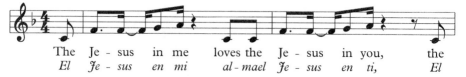

The Je - sus in me loves the Je - sus in you, the
El Je - sus en mi al - mael Je - sus en ti, El

WORDS: Anonymous
MUSIC: Anonymous, arr. by Cynthia Wilson
Arr. © 2007 Abingdon Press, admin. by The Copyright Co.

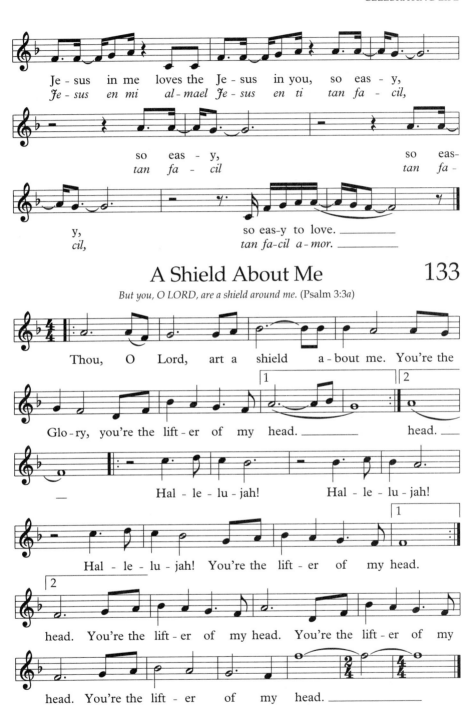

Je - sus in me loves the Je - sus in you, so eas - y,
Je - sus en mi al - mael Je - sus en ti tan fa - cil,

so eas - y, so eas-
tan fa - cil tan fa -

y, so eas-y to love. _____
cil, tan fa-cil a - mor. _____

A Shield About Me 133

But you, O LORD, are a shield around me. (Psalm 3:3a)

Thou, O Lord, art a shield a - bout me. You're the

Glo - ry, you're the lift - er of my head. _____ head. __

__ Hal - le - lu - jah! Hal - le - lu - jah!

Hal - le - lu - jah! You're the lift - er of my head.

head. You're the lift - er of my head. You're the lift - er of my

head. You're the lift - er of my head. _____

WORDS: Donn Thomas and Charles Williams
MUSIC: Donn Thomas and Charles Williams, arr. by Willam S. Moon

134

God Is

God said to Moses, "I AM WHO I AM." (Exodus 3:14a)

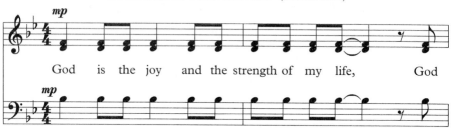

God is the joy and the strength of my life, God

moves all pain, mis - er - y, and strife, God

prom-ised to keep me, nev - er to leave me, God's

nev - er, ev - er come short of his word. I've got to

WORDS: Dr. Robert J. Fryson
MUSIC: Dr. Robert J. Fryson, arr. by Mark A. Miller
Music © 1976 GIA Publications, Inc.

GOD IS
Irr.

135 Goin' Up Yonder

For the perishable body must put on imperishability,
and this mortal body must put on immortality. (1 Corinthians 15:53)

1. If you wan-na know _____ where I'm go - ing, ___
2. I can take the pain, _____ the heart-aches they bring, ___

— — where I'm go - ing _____
— the com-fort's there in know-ing _____ I'll soon be

soon. _____ If an - y-bod - y asks you ___
gone. _____ As God gives me grace, _____ I'll

where I'm go-ing, ___ where I'm go-ing ___
run this race, _____ un - till I see my Sav-ior ___ face to

Refrain

soon. I'm go-ing up yon - der! __ I'm
face.

go-ing up yon - der! __ I'm go-ing up yon - der _

__ to be with my Lord. Oh, I'm go-ing up yon - der! __

I'm go-ing up yon - der! __ I'm

go-ing up yon - der __ to be with my Lord. _____

WORDS: Walter Hawkins
MUSIC: Walter Hawkins, arr. by William S. Moon

Soon and Very Soon

136

"See, I am coming soon; my reward is with me,
to repay according to everyone's work." (Revelation 22:12)

1. Soon and ver - y soon, __ we are going to see the King; __
2. No more cry - ing there, __ we are going to see the King; __
3. No more dy - ing there, __ we are going to see the King; __

soon and ver - y soon, __ we are going - to see the King; __
no more cry - ing there, __ we are going to see the King; __
no more dy - ing there, __ we are going to see the King; __

soon and ver - y soon, __ we are going to see the King; __
no more cry - ing there, __ we are going to see the King; __ Hal-le -
no more dy - ing there, __ we are going to see the King; __

lu - jah! Hal-le - lu - jah! We're going to see the King. __

WORDS: Andraé Crouch
MUSIC: Andraé Crouch, arr. by William S. Moon

VERY SOON
Irregular

137   O I Want to See Him

For now we see in a mirror dimly, but then we will see face to face. (1 Corinthians 13:12*a*)

1. As I jour-ney through the land sing - ing as I go,
2. When in ser-vice for my Lord dark may be the night,
3. When in val-leys low I look toward the moun-tain height,
4. When be-fore me bil - lows rise from the might - y deep,

point - ing souls to Cal - va - ry — to the crim - son flow,
but I'll cling more close to him, he will give me light;
and be-hold my Sav - ior there, lead - ing in the fight,
then my Lord di - rects my bark; he doth safe - ly keep,

man - y ar - rows pierce my soul from with - out, with-in;
Sa-tan's snares may vex my soul, turn my thoughts a - side;
with a ten - der hand out-stretched toward the val - ley low,
and he leads me gen - tly on through this world be-low;

but my Lord leads me on, through him I must win.
but my Lord goes a-head, leads what-e'er be - tide.
guid-ing me I can see, as I on - ward go.
he's a real friend to me, O I love him so.

WORDS: Rufus H. Cornelius
MUSIC: Rufus H. Cornelius

Refrain

O I want to see him, look up-on his face,
there to sing for-ev - er of his sav - ing grace;
grace, his sav-ing grace;
on the streets of Glo - ry let me lift my voice;
cares all past, home at last, ev - er to re-joice.

138 He'll Understand and Say "Well Done"

His lord said unto him, "Well done, good and faithful servant." (Matthew 25:23a KJV)

1. If when you give the best of your ser - vice,
2. Mis - un - der - stood, the Sav - ior of sin - ners,
3. If when this life of la - bor is end - ed,
4. But if you try and fail in your try - ing,

tell - ing the world that the Sav - ior is come;
hung on the cross; he was God's on - ly Son;
and the re - ward of the race you have run;
hands sore and scarred from the work you've be - gun;

be not dis - mayed when men don't be - lieve you;
oh! hear him call - ing his Fa - ther in heaven,
oh! the sweet rest pre - pared for the faith - ful
take up your cross, run quick - ly to meet him;

WORDS: Lucie E. Campbell
MUSIC: Lucie E. Campbell, arr. by Evelyn Simpson-Curenton
Arr. © 2000 GIA Publications, Inc.

WELL DONE
10 10 10 8 with Refrain

he'll un-der-stand; and say, "Well done."
"Not my will, but thine be done."
will be his blest and fi - nal "Well done."
he'll un - der-stand, and say, "Well done."

Refrain

Oh, when I come to the end of my jour-ney, wea-ry of life and the

bat - tle is won; car - ry-ing the staff and the

cross of re - demp-tion, he'll un-der-stand and say, "Well done."

139 Some Day

*Yes, we do have confidence, and we would rather be away from the body
and at home with the Lord.* (2 Corinthians 5:8)

1. Beams of heav - en, as I go, through this
2. Of - ten - times my sky is clear, joy a -
3. Hard - er yet may be the fight, right may
4. Bur - dens now may crush me down, dis - ap -

wil - der - ness be - low, guide my feet in peace - ful
bounds with - out a tear, though a day so bright be -
of - ten yield to might, wick - ed - ness a - while may
point - ments all a - round, trou - bles speak in mourn - ful

ways, turn my mid - nights in - to days; when in the
gun, clouds may hide to - mor - row's sun. There'll be a
reign, Sa - tan's cause may seem to gain; there is a
sigh, sor - row through a tear-stained eye; there is a

dark - ness I would grope, faith al - ways sees a star of
day that's al - ways bright, a day that nev - er yields to -
God that rules a - bove, with hand of pow'r and heart of
world where plea - sure reigns, no mourn - ing soul shall roam its

WORDS: Charles A. Tindley
MUSIC: Charles A. Tindley, arr. by F. A. Clark

SOMEDAY
77.77.88.96 with Refrain

hope, and soon from all life's grief and dan-ger, I shall be
night, and in its light the streets of glo-ry I shall be-
love, if I am right, he'll fight my bat-tle, I shall have
plains, and to that land of peace and glo-ry I want to

Refrain

free some day.
hold some day.
peace some day.
go some day.

I do not know how long 'twill

be, nor what the fu-ture holds for me, but this I

know, if Je-sus leads me, I shall get home some day.

140   If I Can Help Somebody

Therefore, my beloved, be steadfast, immovable, always excelling in the work of the Lord,
because you know that in the Lord your labor is not in vain. (1 Corinthians 15:58)

1. If I can help some-bod-y as I pass a-
2. If I can point some-bod-y to the Lamb once
3. If I can do my du-ty as a Chris-tian

long, if I can cheer some-bod-y with a word or
slain, if I can tell some-bod-y that he rose a-
ought, if I can bring back beau-ty to a world up-

song, if I can show some-bod-y who is trav-eling
gain, that he can cleanse the guilt-y, he can wash the
wrought, if I can spread love's mes-sage that the Mas-ter

wrong,
stain, then my liv-ing shall not be in vain. ____
taught,

Chorus

Then my liv-ing shall not be in vain, ____ then my

liv-ing shall not be in vain, ____ if I can

help some-bod-y as I pass a-long, then my

liv-ing shall not be in vain. ____

WORDS: A. Bazel Androzzo
MUSIC: A. Bazel Androzzo, arr. by Kenneth Morris
© 1958 Boosey & Hawkes

Guide My Feet

141

Guide our feet into the way of peace. (Luke 1:79b)

1. Guide my feet
2. Hold my hand
3. Stand by me
4. I'm your child

while I run this race,

Oh, Lord,

Guide my feet
Hold my hand
Stand by me
I'm your child

while I run this race,

Oh, Lord,

Guide my feet
Hold my hand
Stand by me
I'm your child

while I run this race, for I

vain.

don't want to run this race in vain, race in vain.

vain.

WORDS: African American spiritual
MUSIC: African American spiritual, harm. by Dr. Wendell P. Whalum

142   Come, Come! Ev'rybody Come!

"If you have judged me to be faithful to the Lord, come and stay at my home." (Acts 16:15b)

Come, come! Ev - 'ry - bod - y, come!

Come, come, God loves you ev - 'ry - one.

1. Let your hearts be o - pen; let your hands be free;
2. Let the Ho - ly Spir - it fill you with Sha - lom.

read - y to be lov - ing to all hu - man - i - ty.
Love and peace, re - joic - ing cre - ate the heaven - ly home.

Let your hearts be o - pen; let your hands be free;
Let the Ho - ly Spir - it fill you with Sha - lom.

read - y to be lov - ing to all hu - man - i - ty.
Love and peace, re - joic - ing cre - ate the heaven - ly home.

WORDS: Marilyn E. Thornton
MUSIC: Marilyn E. Thornton
© 2001 Marilyn E. Thornton

143   Welcome into this Place

Lift up your heads, O gates! and be lifted up, O ancient doors!
that the King of glory may come in. (Psalm 24:9)

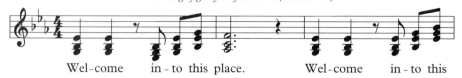

Wel - come in - to this place. Wel - come in - to this

WORDS: Orlando Juarez
MUSIC: Orlando Juarez, arr. by Jimmie Abbington and Darryl Glenn Nettles
© 1991 CMI-HP Publishing, admin. by Word Music, LLC/Life Spring Music

bro - ken ves - sel. You de-sire to a-bide in the

prais-es of your peo - ple, so we lift our hands and we

lift our hearts as we of-fer up this praise un-to your name.

Lord, You Are Welcome   144

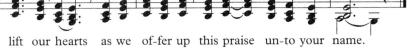

So he hurried down and was happy to welcome him. (Luke 19:6)

1. Lord, you are wel - come in this place.
2. Send your a - noint - ing in this place.
3. Move by your Spir - it in this place.
4. Heal and de - liv - er in this place.

Lord, you are wel-come in this place. Lord, you are
Send your a - noint-ing in this place. Send your a -
Move by your Spir - it in this place. Move by your
Heal and de - liv - er in this place. Heal and de -

| 1–3 | 2 | 4 |

wel-come in this place. Have your way.
noint-ing in this place. Have your way.
Spir - it in this place. Have your way.
liv - er in this place. Have your way.

WORDS: Kurt Lykes
MUSIC: Kurt Lykes, arr. by Cynthia Wilson

145   Here I Am to Worship

O come, let us worship and bow down, let us kneel before the LORD, our Maker! (Psalm 95:6)

1. Light of the world, you stepped down in-to dark-ness,
2. King of all days, oh, so high-ly ex-alt-ed,

o - pen my eyes let me _____ see
glo - rious in heav - en a - bove.

beau - ty that made this heart a - dore you,
Hum - bly you came to the earth you cre - at - ed,

hope of a life spent with __ you.
all for love's sake be - came _ poor.

So here I am to

wor - ship; here I am to bow down; here I am to

say that you're my God. __ And you're al - to - geth - er

Third time to Coda ⊕

love - ly, al-to-geth-er wor-thy, al-to-geth-er won-der-ful to me. _

WORDS: Tim Hughes
MUSIC: Tim Hughes, arr. by Cynthia Wilson

© 2001 Kingsman's Thankyou Music (PRS), worldwide admin. by EMI CMG Publishing,
excluding Europe which is admin. by Kingswaysongs.com

146   Just One Word from You

One does not live by bread alone,
but by every word that comes from the mouth of the LORD. (Deuteronomy 8:3b)

Let me not be just a hear - er of your

Word. Let your Word not fall up - on ston - y

ground. But may it find a rest-ing place in my heart, that I might

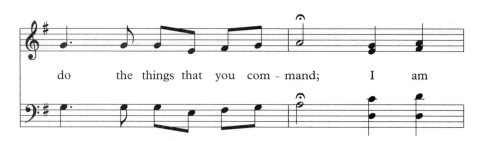

do the things that you com - mand; I am

WORDS: Eli Wilson, Jr.
MUSIC: Eli Wilson, Jr.

147 God Is Here

"Come to me, all you that are weary and are carrying heavy burdens, and I will give you rest." (Matthew 11:28)

There is a sweet a-noint-ing in this sanc-tu-ar-y, there is a still-ness in the at-mos-phere, come and lay down the bur-dens you have car-ried, for in this sanc-tu-ar-y God is here. God is here, God is here, to break the yoke and lift the heav-y bur-den. God is here, God is here, to

WORDS: Martha D. Munizzi, Israel Houghton, and Meleasa Houghton
MUSIC: Martha D. Munizzi, Israel Houghton, and Meleasa Houghton

heal the hope - less heart and bless the bro - ken.

Come and lay down the bur-dens you have car - ried for

in this sanc - tu - ar - y God is here. ____

Jesu Tawa Pano/Jesus, We Are Here 148

When the day of Pentecost had come, they were all together in one place. (Acts 2:1)

Je - su ta - wa pa - no; Je - su ta - wa pa - no;
Je - sus, we are here; Je - sus, we are here;

Solo *Ma-mbo Je-su.

Je-su ta-wa pa-no; ta-wa pa-no, mu zi - ta re-nyu.
Je-sus, we are here; we are here for you.

Omit last time.

Shona Transliteration:
   Yah-zoo tah-wah pah-no
   tah-wah pah-no, moo zee-tah ray-noo

WORDS: Patrick Matsikenyiri (Zimbabwe)
MUSIC: Patrick Matsikenyiri
© 1990, 1996 General Board of Global Ministries, GBGMusik.

MATSIKENYIRI
Irregular

149   Standin' in the Need of Prayer

Give praise, O servants of the LORD, you that stand in the house of the LORD,
in the courts of the house of our God. (Psalm 135:1b, 2)

1. Not my broth-er, not my sis - ter, but it's me, O Lord,
2. Not the preach-er, not the dea - con, but it's me, O Lord,
3. Not my fa - ther, nor my moth - er, but it's me, O Lord,
4. Not the stran-ger, nor my neigh-bor, but it's me, O Lord,

Response ... *Leader*

stand - in' in the need of prayer; not my
stand - in' in the need of prayer; not the
stand - in' in the need of prayer; not my
stand - in' in the need of prayer; not the

broth - er, nor my sis - ter, but it's me, O Lord,
preach-er, nor the dea - con, but it's me, O Lord,
fa - ther, nor my moth - er, but it's me, O Lord,
stran - ger, nor my neigh-bor, but it's me, O Lord,

Response

stand - in' in the need of prayer.
stand - in' in the need of prayer.
stand - in' in the need of prayer.
stand - in' in the need of prayer.

WORDS: African American spiritual
MUSIC: African American spiritual
Arr. © 1981 Abingdon Press, admin. by The Copyright Co.

It's me

it's me, it's me, O Lord, stand-in' in the need of prayer;

It's me

it's me, it's me, O Lord, stand-in' in the need of prayer;

Early in the Morning   150

O God, you are my God, I seek you, my soul thirsts for you. (Psalm 63:1a)

Ear-ly in the morn - ing ____ I will seek your face.

Long-ing for your fav - or, ____ thirst-ing for your grace,

clear-ing all the clut - ter ____ be-fore the day be-gins,

I in-vite you in, my God, my

| To repeat | Song ending |

King. ____ Ear - ly in the King. ____

WORDS: Johnetta Johnson Page
MUSIC: Johnetta Johnson Page

151 Living in the Imagination of God

"What no eye has seen, nor ear heard, nor the human heart conceived,
what God has prepared for those who love him." (1 Corinthians 2:9)

WORDS: Cecilia Olusola Tribble
MUSIC: Cecilia Olusola Tribble

© 2007 Cecilia Olusola Tribble

152   Walking Up the King's Highway

I will make them strong in the LORD, and they shall walk in his name. (Zechariah 10:12)

1. My way gets bright-er, my load gets light-er,
2. Don't have to wor-ry, don't have to hur-ry,
3. If you're not walk-ing, start while I'm talk-ing,

walk-ing up the King's high - way,

there's joy in know-ing
Christ walks be-side me
there'll be a bless-ing

with God I'm go - ing,
an - gels to guide me, walk-ing up the King's high - way.
you'll be pos-sess - ing,

Refrain

It's a high - way to heav - en, none can walk up there

WORDS: Mary Gardner and Thomas Dorsey
MUSIC: Mary Gardner and Thomas Dorsey, arr. by Monya Davis Logan

KING'S HIGHWAY
55 7 55 7 with Refrain

153 Holy Is His Name

Having become as much superior to angels
as the name he has inherited is more excellent than theirs. (Hebrews 1:4)

WORDS: Leon Lewis
MUSIC: Leon Lewis

154 Hold to God's Unchanging Hand

For I, the LORD your God, hold your right hand;
it is I who say to you, "Do not fear, I will help you." (Isaiah 41:13)

1. Time is filled with swift tran - si - tion.
2. Trust in him who will not leave you.
3. Cov - et not this world's vain rich - es
4. When your jour - ney is com - plet - ed,

Naught of earth un - moved can stand.
What - so - ev - er years may bring.
that so ra - pid - ly de - cay.
if to God you have been true.

Build your hopes on things e - ter - nal. ___
If by earth - ly friends for - sak - en, ___
Seek to gain the heaven - ly trea - sures. _
fair and bright the home in glo - ry ___

Hold to God's un - chang - ing hand. _
still more close - ly to him cling. _
They will nev - er pass a - way. ___
your en - rap - tured soul will view. ___

WORDS: Jennie Wilson
MUSIC: F. L. Eiland, arr. by Stephen Key
Arr. © 2000 GIA Publications, Inc.

UNCHANGING HAND
87 87 with Refrain

Hold to his hand, _ God's un-chang-ing hand. _

Hold to his hand, _ God's un-chang-ing hand. _

Build your hopes on things e - ter - nal. __

Hold to God's un-chang-ing hand. _____

155 Heavenly Father

For if you fogive others their trespasses,
your heavenly Father will also forgive you. (Matthew 6:14)

Heav-en-ly Fa - ther, Lord, I need _

Heav-en-ly Fa -

_ you in my life, in my life.

ther, Lord, I need ____ you in my life, in my

life. Heav-en-ly Fa - ther, Lord, I need _ you in my

WORDS: Frederick Burchell
MUSIC: Frederick Burchell and Walter Hill, transcribed by William S. Moon
© 2005 B4 Entertainment

Lord, Listen to Your Children Praying 156

"From the lips of children and infants you have ordained praise." (Matthew 21:16b NIV)

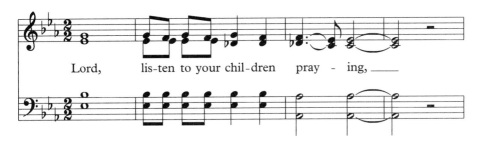

Lord, lis-ten to your chil-dren pray - ing, ____

Lord, send your Spir-it in this place; ____

Lord, lis-ten to your chil-dren pray - ing, ____ send us

love, send us power, send us grace. ____

WORDS: Ken Medema
MUSIC: Ken Medema
© 1973 Hope Publishing Co.

CHILDREN PRAYING
98.99

157 Precious Jesus

*For I am not ashamed of the gospel; it is the power of God for salvation to everyone
who has faith, to the Jew first and also to the Greek. (Romans 1:16)*

Pre - cious Je - sus, how I love you, how I

lift high my voice with your praise. Ho - ly

Spir - it, I im - plore thee, drench my

[1] heart as my lips 'part your grace. [2] Pre - cious grace.

I am per - suad - ed, Lord, to love you.

I have been changed to bless your name.

WORDS: Thomas A. Whitfield
MUSIC: Thomas A. Whitfield, arr. by William S. Moon
Arr. © 2007 Abingdon Press, admin. by The Copyright Co.

I am con - strained by the great gos - pel, for -
wor - ship
ev - er to wor - ship thee.

Remember Me 158

Remember not the sins of my youth, nor my transgressions;
according to thy mercy remember thou me for thy goodness' sake, O LORD. (Psalm 25:7 KJV)

Re - mem - ber me, re - mem - ber
me, O Lord, re - mem - ber me.

WORDS: Trad.
MUSIC: Trad., harm. by J. Jefferson Cleveland

159 Thy Way, O Lord

Thy kingdom come. Thy will be done in earth, as it is in heaven. (Matthew 6:10 KJV)

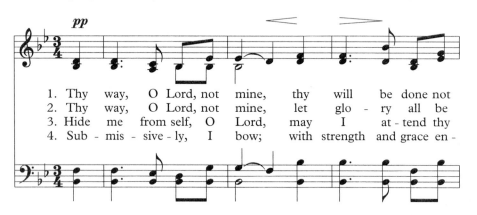

1. Thy way, O Lord, not mine, thy will be done not
2. Thy way, O Lord, not mine, let glo - ry all be
3. Hide me from self, O Lord, may I at - tend thy
4. Sub - mis - sive - ly, I bow; with strength and grace en -

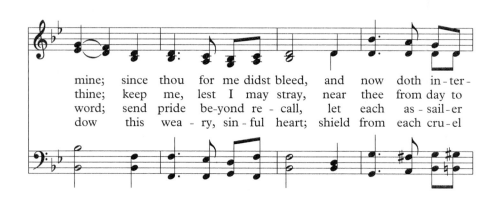

mine; since thou for me didst bleed, and now doth in - ter -
thine; keep me, lest I may stray, near thee from day to
word; send pride be - yond re - call, let each as - sail - er
dow this wea - ry, sin - ful heart; shield from each cru - el

cede, each day I sim - ply plead, thy
day; teach me to watch and pray, thy
fall, be thou my all in all, thy
dart; may I from thee ne'er part, thy

WORDS: Nina B. Jackson
MUSIC: E. C. Deas, arr. by Darryl Glenn Nettles
Arr. © 2007 Abingdon Press, admin. by The Copyright Co.

THY WAY
66 666 4 with Refrain

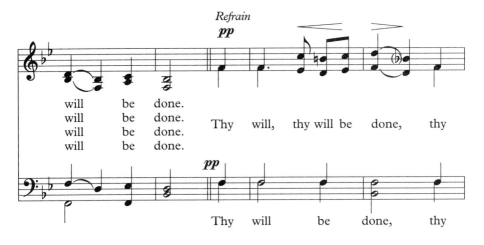

Refrain

will be done.
will be done.
will be done.
will be done.

Thy will, thy will be done, thy

Thy will be done, thy

will, thy will be done; in - cline my heart each

will be done;

day to say, "Thy will be done." A - men.

160 You Are the One

O Lord, all my longing is known to you;
my sighing is not hidden from you. (Psalm 38:9)

You are the One who sees me. You are the

One who hears me when I call. E-ven when I

run a - way from you, you still speak my name

call - ing me back to you. You are the

One who sees me. You are the

One who hears me when I call. E-ven when I

run a - way from you, you still speak my name

WORDS: Jonathan Cole Dow and Johnetta Johnson Page
MUSIC: Jonathan Cole Dow and Johnetta Johnson Page, arr. by William S. Moon

161 He's Sweet, I Know

How sweet are your words to my taste, sweeter than honey to my mouth! (Psalm 119:103)

Refrain He's sweet, I know. He's sweet, I
1. I can't for - get when I was
2. I have my tick - et here in my

know. Storm clouds may rise, strong winds may
sad. Head hang - ing down, soul feel - ing
hand. I'm go - ing to that beau - ti - ful

blow. I'll tell the world wher-
bad. All I could say was
land. Some - time I weep and

ev - er I go. That I've found a
Lord take my heart. __ Je - sus heard and
some - time I moan. But I'm bound for

WORDS: Trad. Gospel hymn
MUSIC: Trad. Gospel hymn, arr. by Kenneth Louis and Nolan Williams, Jr.
Arr. © 2000 GIA Publications, Inc.

HE'S SWEET
88 9 11

Sav - ior, and he's sweet, I know.
saved me, and gave me a start.
glo - ry, and I'm go - ing on.

You Are Holy 162

Holy, holy, holy, the Lord God the Almighty, who was and is and is to come. (Revelation 4:8c)

Very slowly

1. You are ho - ly, ____ ho - ly, ho - ly. ____ You are
(2. You are) faith - ful, ____ faith - ful, faith - ful. ____ You are
(3. You are) righ - teous, _ righ-teous, righ - teous. _ You are
(4. You are) ho - ly, ____ ho - ly, ho - ly. ____ You are

ho - ly, ____ ho - ly, Lord. ____ You are ho - ly, ____
faith - ful, ____ faith - ful, Lord. ____ You are faith - ful, ____
righ - teous, _ righ - teous, Lord. ____ You are righ - teous, _
ho - ly, ____ ho - ly, Lord. ____ You are ho - ly, ____

__ ho - ly, ho - ly. ____ You are ho - ly, ho -
__ faith - ful, faith - ful. ____ You are faith - ful, faith -
__ righ-teous, righ - teous. _ You are righ - teous, righ -
__ ho - ly, ho - ly. ____ You are ho - ly, ho -

1–3 **4**

ly. ____ 2. You are
ful. ____ 3. You are
teous. ____ 4. You are
ly. ____ __ A - men. ____

WORDS: Cecilia L. Clemons
MUSIC: Cecilia L. Clemons

163 Just a Little Talk with Jesus

It is Christ Jesus, who did, yes, who was raised,
who is at the right hand of God, who indeed intercedes for us. (Romans 8:34*b*)

1. I once was lost in sin but Je-sus took me in,
2. Some-times my path seems drear, with-out a ray of cheer,
3. I may have doubts and fears, my eyes be filled with tears,

and then a lit-tle light from heav-en filled my soul;
and then a cloud of doubt may hide the light of day;
but Je-sus is a friend who watch-es day and night;

it bathed my heart in love and wrote my name a-bove,
the mists of sin may rise and hide the star-ry skies,
I go to him in prayer, he knows my ev-ery care,

Refrain

and just a lit-tle talk with Je-sus made me whole.
but just a lit-tle talk with Je-sus clears the way.
and just a lit-tle talk with Je-sus makes it right.

Now let us

WORDS: Cleavant Derricks
MUSIC: Ceavant Derricks

JUST A LITTLE TALK
66 12 66 12 with refrain

164 Stand by Me

But God's firm foundation stands, bearing this inscription:
"The Lord knows those who are his." (2 Timothy 2:19a)

Reverently, moderate speed

1. When the storms of life are rag-ing,
2. In the midst of trib - u - la-tion,
3. In the midst of faults and fail-ures, stand by me;
4. In the midst of per - se - cu-tion,
5. When I'm grow-ing old and fee - ble,

when the storms of life are rag-ing, When the
in the midst of trib - u - la-tion, When the
in the midst of faults and fail-ures, stand by me. When I
in the midst of per - se - cu-tion, When my
When I'm grow-ing old and fee - ble, When my

world is toss - ing me like a ship up - on the sea;
hosts of hell as - sail, and my strength be-gins to fail,
do the best I can, and my friends mis - un - der - stand,
foes in bat - tle ar - ray un - der - take to stop my way,
life be - comes a bur - den and I'm near - ing chil - ly Jor-dan,

WORDS: Charles Albert Tindley
MUSIC: Charles Albert Tindley, arr. by J. Jefferson Cleveland and Verolga Nix
Arr. © 1981 Abingdon Press, admin. by The Copyright Co.

thou who   rul - est wind and wa - ter,
thou who   nev - er lost a bat - tle,
thou who   know-est all a - bout me, stand by me.
thou who   sav - ed Paul and Si - las,
O thou   "Lil - ly of the Val - ley,"

Sanctuary   165

*May the God of peace himself sanctify you entirely; and may your spirit and soul and body
be kept sound and blameless at the coming of our Lord Jesus Christ.* (1 Thessalonians 5:23)

Slowly

Lord, pre - pare me to be a sanc-tu - ar - y, pure and

ho - ly, tried and true; with thanks-giv - ing, I'll be a

liv - ing sanc-tu - ar - y for you.

WORDS: John Thompson and Randy Scruggs
MUSIC: John Thompson and Randy Scruggs
© 1982 Full Armor Music and Whole Armor Music

SANCTUARY
Irregular

166   Somebody Prayed for Me

Pray for one another, so that you may be healed. (James 5:16*b*)

*Use "she" on verse two as appropriate.

WORDS: Dorothy Norwood and Alvin Darling
MUSIC: Dorothy Norwood and Alvin Darling

© 1991 Malaco Music Co. (BMI)/Kosciusko Music (SESAC)

Learning to Lean

Trust in the LORD with all thine heart;
and lean not unto thine own understanding. (Proverbs 3:5 KJV)

Learn-ing to lean, learn-ing to lean, I'm
learn-ing to lean on Je - sus.
Find-ing more pow-er than I've ev-er seen. I'm
learn-ing to lean on Je - sus.

WORDS: John Stallings
MUSIC: John Stallings, arr. by Evelyn Simpson-Curenton

168 We'll Understand It Better By and By

Now I know only in part; then I will know fully,
even as I have been fully known. (1 Corinthians 13:12b)

WORDS: Charles Albert Tindley
MUSIC: Charles Albert Tindley, arr. by Theodore Thomas
Arr. © 2007 Abingdon Press, admin. by The Copyright Co.

BY AND BY
77 15 77 11 with Refrain

land   of   per - fect   day,   when   the
trust - ing   in   the   Lord,   and   ac -
guides   us   with his   eye,   and   we'll
won - der why   the   test,   when   we

mists have rolled a - way,   we will un-der-stand it bet-ter by and
cord - ing   to God's word, we will un-der-stand it bet-ter by and
fol - low   till lwe   die,   we will un-der-stand it bet-ter by and
try   to   do our   best,   but we'll un-der-stand it bet-ter by and

by.   By   and   by   when the morn-ing comes,

when   the saints of   God are gath-ered home, we'll tell   the sto - ry

how we o - ver-come, for we'll un-der-stand it bet-ter by and by.

169   We Offer Christ

For we do not proclaim ourselves; we proclaim Jesus Christ as Lord
and ourselves as your slaves for Jesus' sake. (2 Corinthians 4:5)

We of-fer Christ to you, oh, my broth-er, we of - fer Christ to you, oh, my sis - ter. He will give you brand new life through life a - bun - dant-ly; oh come, come on ___ to Christ. _

WORDS: Joel Britton
MUSIC: Joel Britton, arr. by Valeria A. Foster

Praise You

*And it is no longer I who live, but it is Christ who lives in me. And the life I now live in the flesh
I live by faith in the Son of God, who loved me and gave himself for me.* (Galatians 2:20)

WORDS: Elizabeth Goodine
MUSIC: Elizabeth Goodine

© 1993 New Spring Publishing (ASCAP), a div. of Brentwood-Benson Music Publishing, Inc.

171 Come unto Jesus

"Come to me, all you that are weary and are carrying heavy burdens,
and I will give you rest." (Matthew 11:28)

WORDS: Raymond Wise
MUSIC: Raymond Wise

© 1991 Raise Publishing Company

172   Yes, God Is Real

For I know that my Redeemer lives, and that at the last he will stand upon the earth. (Job 19:25)

1. There are some things   I may not know,
2. Some folks may doubt,   some folks may scorn,
3. I can-not tell   just how you felt

there are some plac - es I can-not go,
all can de - sert and leave me a - lone,
when Je - sus took your sins a - way,

but I am sure of this one thing,
but as for me I'll take God's part,
but since that day, yes, since that hour,

that God is real for I can feel him deep with-in.
for God is real and I can feel him in my heart.
God has been real for I can feel his ho - ly power.

Yes, God is real, he's real in my soul;
yes, God is real for he has washed and made me whole;

his love for me is like pure gold, yes, God is
reall for I can feel him in my soul.

WORDS: Kenneth Morris
MUSIC: Kenneth Morris, arr. by Oscar Dismuke

GOD IS REAL
8 9 8 12 with Refrain

© 1994 (Renewed) Martin and Morris, arr. © 2006 Martin and Morris, admin. by Unichappell Music, Inc.

Lead Me, Guide Me

173

Teach me thy way, O LORD, and lead me in a plain path. (Psalm 27:11 KJV)

Lead me, guide me, a - long the way, for if you
lead me, I can - not stray. Lord, let me walk each
day with thee. Lead me, O Lord, lead me. _____

Fine

1. I am weak and I need thy strength and
2. Help me tread in the paths of righ - teous -
3. I am lost if you take your hand from

power to help me o - ver my weak - est
ness, be my aid when Sa - tan and sin op -
me, I am blind with - out thy Light to

hour. Help me through the dark - ness thy face to
press. I am put - ting all my trust in
see, Lord, just al - ways let me thy ser - vant

D.C.

see, Lead me, O Lord, lead me. _____
thee. Lead me, O Lord, lead me. _____
be. Lead me, O Lord, lead me. _____

WORDS: Doris Akers
MUSIC: Doris Akers

LEAD ME, GUIDE ME
Irregular with Refrain

174 Center of My Joy

And not only so, but we also joy in God through our Lord Jesus Christ,
by whom we have now received the atonement. (Romans 5:11 KJV)

WORDS: Gloria Gaither
MUSIC: Richard Smallwood, William Gaither, arr. by Mark A. Miller

CENTER OF MY JOY
Irregular

I'm Determined

175

Beloved, I do not consider that I have made it my own, but this one thing I do: forgetting
what lies behind and straining forward to what lies ahead, I press on. (Philippians 3:13-14a)

Each section can be repeated as desired.

WORDS: African American trad.
MUSIC: African American trad., arr. by Marilyn E. Thornton
Arr. © 2007 Abingdon Press, admin. by The Copyright Co.

176   I Love the Lord

I love the LORD, because he has heard my voice and my supplications. (Psalm 116:1)

WORDS: Richard Smallwood
MUSIC: Richard Smallwood, arr. by Nolan Williams, Jr.

has - ten to his throne.   I'll   has - ten to his   throne.

I Will Bow to You   177

*"But if not, be it known to you, O king, that we will not serve your gods
and we will not worship the golden statue that you have set up."* (Daniel 3:18)

Lord,   I will bow   to   you,   to no oth - er   God _

_ but you   a-lone. _   Lord, I will wor - ship you,

noth-ing hands have made _ but you   a-lone. _   I will lay _

_ down my i - dols,   thrones I   have made,

all that has tak - en   my heart. _   Lord, I will bow   to you,

to no oth - er God _   but you   a-lone. _

WORDS: Pete Episcopo
MUSIC: Pete Episcopo, arr. by Mark A. Miller

178   Change My Heart, O God

Yet, O LORD, you are our Father; we are the clay, and you are our potter;
we are all the work of your hand. (Isaiah 64:8)

Change my heart, O God, _   make it ev-er true. _

Change my heart, O God, _   may I be like you. _

You are the Pot - ter,   I am the clay. _

Mold me an make me,   this is what I pray.

Change my heart, O God, _   make it ev-er true. _

Change my heart, O God, _   may I be like you. _

WORDS: Eddie Espinosa
MUSIC: Eddie Espinosa

CHANGE MY HEART
Irregular

Optional D.S. ending   *D.S.*‖ *Song ending*   ‖ *Optional choral ending*

rit.

Change my heart, O   God,   may I be like   you. ____

God Has Done Great Things for Me   179

The LORD has done great things for us, and we rejoiced. (Psalm 126:3)

1. *He   has   done great things   for   me. ___   Great   things,
2. He   has made   a   way   for   me. ___   Made   a   way,
3. He   will   give   you vic - to - ry. ____   Vic - to - ry,
4. I'm gon-na be   a   wit-ness for him. ___   Wit - ness,
5. I'm gon-na let   my   lit - tle light shine. _   Shine,

great   things.   He   has   done great things   for   me. __
made   a   way.   He   has made   a   way   for   me. __
vic - to - ry.   He   will   give   you vic - to - ry. ___
wit - ness.   I'm gon-na be   a   wit-ness for him. _
shine.   I'm gon-na let   my   lit - tle light shine. _

*May substitute "God."

WORDS: Jessy Dixon   GREAT THINGS
MUSIC: Jessy Dixon, arr. by Stephen Key   7.4.7
© Dixon Music, Inc.; arr. © 2000 GIA Publications, Inc.

180   Completely Yes

And she answered and said unto him, "Yes, Lord." (Mark 7:28a KJV)

WORDS: Sandra Crouch
MUSIC: Sandra Crouch, arr. by Stephen Key

"Yes, yes, yes! Yes, Lord!" From the bot-tom of my heart, "Yes, Lord!" To the depths of my soul. "Yes, Lord!"

181   He's My Foundation

Built upon the foundation of the apostles and prophets,
with Christ Jesus himself as the cornerstone. (Ephesians 2:20)

Refrain
No matter what you're facing
He's my foundation.
When storms keep on raging
He's my foundation.
Giver of Salvation
He's my foundation.
That's why I gotta praise him
He's my foundation.

1. When trials and tests
   He's my foundation.
   try to get me at my best
   He's my foundation.
   I still know I'm blessed
   He's my foundation.
   I've built my life on Christ.
   I've built my life on Christ.

2. When this old world
   He's my foundation.
   tries to get me down
   He's my foundation.
   He'll turn it all around,
   He's my foundation.
   I've built my life on Christ.
   I've built my life on Christ.

Refrain

3. When all the pain
   He's my foundation.
   is coming down like rain
   He's my foundation.
   have faith it's gonna change
   He's my foundation.
   I've built my life on Christ.
   I've built my life on Christ.

WORDS: Frederick Burchell

4. When I feel trapped
   He's my foundation.
   And I can't get out
   He's my foundation.
   I'll have faith and won't doubt
   He's my foundation.
   I've built my life on Christ.
   I've built my life on Christ.

Refrain

He's My Foundation
181

Refrain

*Built upon the foundation of the apostles and prophets,
with Christ Jesus himself as the cornerstone.* (Ephesians 2:20)

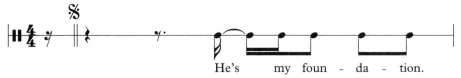

He's   my   foun - da - tion.

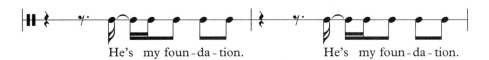

He's my foun - da - tion.   He's my foun - da - tion.

Fine   Verses 1–4

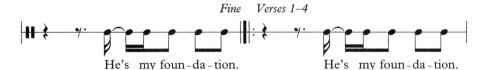

He's my foun - da - tion.   He's my foun - da - tion.

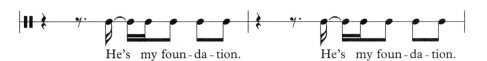

He's my foun - da - tion.   He's my foun - da - tion.

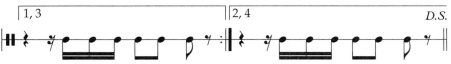

1, 3   2, 4   D.S.

I've built my life on Christ.   I've built my life on Christ.

WORDS: Frederick Burchell
MUSIC: Frederick Burchell, transcribed by William S. Moon
© 2006 B4 Entertainment

182 The Solid Rock

But it did not fall, because it had been founded on rock. (Matthew 7:25b)

1. My hope is built on noth-ing less than
2. When dark-ness veils his love-ly face, I
3. His oath, his cov - e - nant, his blood, sup -
4. When he shall come with trum-pet sound, O

Je - sus' blood and righ - teous - ness. I
rest on his un - chang-ing grace. In
port me in the whelm-ing flood. When
may I then in him be found. Dressed

dare not trust the sweet-est frame, but
ev - ery high and storm-y gale, my
all a - round my soul gives way, he
in his righ - teous - ness a - lone, fault -

Refrain

whol-ly lean on Je - sus' name.
an - chor holds with-in the veil. On Christ the sol - id
then is all my hope and stay.
less to stand be - fore the throne.

rock I stand, all oth-er ground is sink-ing sand, all

oth-er ground is sink-ing sand. _____

WORDS: Edward Mote
MUSIC: William B. Bradbury, arr. Johnetta Johnson Page and Jonathan Cole Dow
THE SOLID ROCK
LM with Refrain

Yes, Lord, Yes

"I delight to do your will, O my God; your law is within my heart." (Psalm 40:8)

I said, "Yes, Lord, yes!" _ to your will and to your way. _

I say, "Yes, Lord, yes!" _ I will trust you and o-bey. _

When your Spir-it speaks to me, _ with my

whole heart I'll a-gree _ and my an-swer will be yes, Lord, yes! _

1 _ **2** I said _ Lord, yes! _

Lord, yes! _

WORDS: Lynn Keesecker
MUSIC: Lynn Keesecker, arr. by Marilyn E. Thornton

184 You Are My All in All

"I am the Alpha and Omega," says the Lord God,
who is and who was and who is to come, the Almighty. (Revelation 1:8)

1. You are my strength when I am
2. Tak-ing my sin, my cross, my

weak. You are the treas-ure that I seek. You are my all in
shame, ris-ing a-gain I bless your name, you are my all in

all. Seek-ing you as a pre-cious
all. When I fall down you pick me

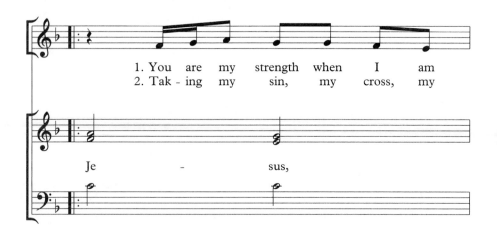

jewel, Lord, to give up I'd be a fool. You are my all in all.
up. When I am dry you fill my cup. You are my all in all.

1. You are my strength when I am
2. Tak-ing my sin, my cross, my

Je - sus,

WORDS: Dennis Jernigan
MUSIC: Dennis Jernigan, arr. by William S. Moon

185   Never Been Scared

So then, brothers and sisters, stand firm and hold fast to the
traditions that you were taught by us. (2 Thessalonians 2:15a)

The Queen of Crunk jumps out and I step in the booth.
And I'm knucking for my faith and only speaking the truth.
God sent his message out with this pad and this pen.
And if you stop what I'm saying then I'll say it again.
We in the church with our hands up. We feeling pumped up.
If you a soldier of Christ, go on and stand up
you got your mug on us, like what we doing over there.
I thought I told you in the chorus that we never been scared.

Be still in the presence but we moving around.
Now take your shoes off, dawg, you on holy ground.
You sit there with your arms crossed and shoulders shrugging.
You claim that you get crunk but you ain't showing me nothing.
So don't talk about it, be about it, walk what you speaking.
I done made up my mind, a righteous life is what I'm seeking.
I'm unbreakable, unmovable, you ain't shaking my faith.
Even though I pleaded guilty, God has pardoned my case.

> *Refrain*
> I'm going to stand up for my faith.
> *I ain't never been scared.*
> Get it crunk up in this place.
> *I ain't never been scared.*
> I bring the gospel to the street.
> *I ain't never been scared,*
> *never been scared, never been scared.*

We keep it crunk, we keep it bouncing, squashing all them doubting.
Telling all them mountains get out of my surrounding.
I'm standing by faith, do whatever it takes.
And I'm rolling with the "G" "O" "D"; that's so great.
See you need to be down, come on and roll with my squad.
See I'm rolling with God, y'all be trying so hard.
Some think we odd, some think we strange.
But see I'm blessed because ya know my life has been changed.

WORDS: David Manning, Jr. and Frederick Burchell
MUSIC: Frederick Burchell, transcribed by William S. Moon

Into a new man I'm walking forth in the ministry.
Devil tried to hinder me 'cause I'm doing outreach.
So watch my praise go up and the blessings come down.
And I'm taking my sound, and spread it all around town.
See the beats be knocking and the lyrics be poppin'
and with God on my side, with me there's no stoppin'.
Never been scared forward, march, here I come
and from a mighty long way God has brought me from.

Refrain

I'm standing up tall my faith don't never shatter.
My clique we rolling thick like boxes of cake batter.
From Alabama to Memphis, from the brick to the burbs.
I'm speaking in metaphors, nouns, and verbs.
I hate tradition like on Monday so I'm pushing it back.
I got the devil breathing hard like an asthma attack.
He thought he had me in his hands but the grace was sufficient.
You wanna get the truth, just turn this up and listen.

See I'm urging my brothers to be a living sacrifice.
To present your bodies as holy unto the Savior, the Christ.
I ain't never been scared to stand up and never been scared to ride.
Ain't never been about me so I'm putting down my pride.
My faith can't be shaken and I'm always ready to rumble, man.
But don't get confused, see I walk as a humble man.
Gonna buck my faith they try to shut me up.
Try to sit me down but I'm standing back up.
I'm going to spit upon this mic and change the game.
Coming up, man, gotta praise his name.

Refrain

185 Never Been Scared

So then, brothers and sisters, stand firm and hold fast to the
traditions that you were taught by us. (2 Thessalonians 2:15a)

Refrain

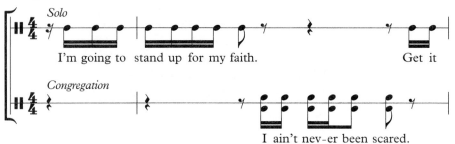

Solo: I'm going to stand up for my faith. Get it

Congregation: I ain't nev-er been scared.

crunk up in this place. I bring the

I ain't nev - er been scared.

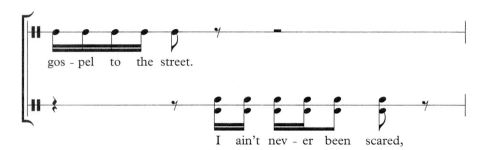

gos - pel to the street.

I ain't nev - er been scared,

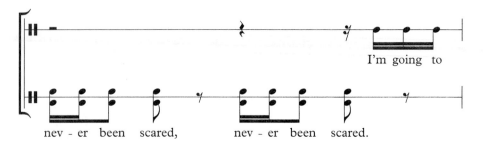

I'm going to

nev - er been scared, nev - er been scared.

WORDS: David Manning, Jr. and Frederick Burchell
MUSIC: Frederick Burchell, transcribed by William S. Moon

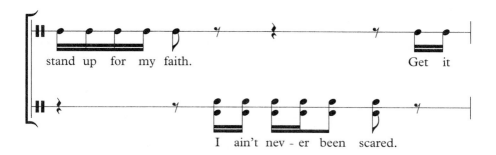

stand up for my faith.   Get it

I ain't nev - er been scared.

crunk up in this place.   I bring the

I ain't nev - er been scared.

gos - pel to the street.

I ain't nev - er been scared,

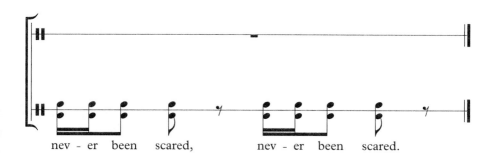

nev - er been scared,   nev - er been scared.

186   I Will Arise

"I will get up and go to my father." (Luke 15:18a)

1. Come, ye sin-ners, poor and need-y, weak and wound-ed, sick and sore; Je-sus read-y stands to save you, full of pit-y, love, and power.
2. Come, ye thirst-y, come, and wel-come, God's free boun-ty glo-ri-fy; true be-lief and true re-pen-tance, ev-ery grace that brings you nigh.
3. Come, ye wea-ry, heav-y-lad-en, lost and ru-ined by the fall; if you tar-ry till you're bet-ter, you will nev-er come at all.

I will a-rise and go to Je-sus, he will em-brace me in his arms; in the arms of my dear Sav-ior, O there are ten thou-sand charms.

WORDS: Joseph Hart
MUSIC: Walker's *Southern Harmony*, 1835

RESTORATION
8 7 8 7 with Refrain

My Soul Loves Jesus

187

I love you, O LORD, my strength. (Psalm 18:1)

1. My soul loves Je - sus, my soul loves
2. He's a won-der in my soul, he's a won-der in my
3. My soul seeks to please him, my soul seeks to

Je - sus, my soul loves Je - sus; bless his name.
soul, he's a won-der in my soul; bless his name.
please him, my soul seeks to please him, bless his name.

— My soul loves Je - sus, my soul loves
— He's a won-der in my soul, he's a won-der in my
— My soul seeks to please him, my soul seeks to

Je - sus, my soul loves Je - sus; bless his name.
soul, he's a won-der in my soul; bless his name.
please him, my soul seeks to please him; bless his name.

WORDS: Charles H. Mason
MUSIC: Charles H. Mason, arr. by Iris Stevenson

MY SOUL LOVES JESUS
Irregular

© 1982 The Church of God in Christ Publishing Board

188 Come, Be Baptized

And people kept coming and were being baptized. (John 3:23b)

1. Come as a child, come to the wa - ters; to the
2. Come as a child, come, sons and daugh-ters, ____

fam - ily of God, come, sons and daugh-ters.
draw from the well life - giv - ing wa - ters.

Come to the riv - er, the Lord, the life - giv - er;
Drink of the riv - er, the Lord, the life - giv - er;

wash in the love that is sent from a - bove.
feel how it pours out the life that is yours.

Refrain

Come, be bap-tized in the name of the Fa - ther.

Come, be bap-tized in the name of the Son. Come, be

WORDS: G. Alan Smith
MUSIC: G. Alan Smith
© 1982 Hope Publishing Co.

COME, BE BAPTIZED
Irregular with Refrain

bap-tized in the name of the Spir-it. Come, be

bap-tized in love. love.

Wade in the Water 189

Moses stretched out his hand over the sea. The LORD drove the sea back
by a strong east wind all night, and turned the sea into dry land. (Exodus 14:21)

Wade in the wa - ter, wade in the wa - ter, chil-dren.

Wade in the wa - ter, God's gon-na trou-ble the wa - ter.

1. See that band all dressed in white. God's gon-na trou-ble the
2. See that band all dressed in red. God's gon-na trou-ble the

wa - ter. The lead - er looks like an
wa - ter. It looks like the chil-dren that

Is - rael - ite. God's gon-na trou-ble the wa - ter.
Mo - ses led. God's gon-na trou-ble the wa - ter.

WORDS: African American Traditional
MUSIC: African American spiritual, arr. by Monya Davis Logan
Arr. © 2007 Abingdon Press, admin. by The Copyright Co.

WADE IN THE WATER
Irregular with Refrain

190   Take Me to the Water

"Look, here is water! What is to prevent me from being baptized?" (Acts 8:37)

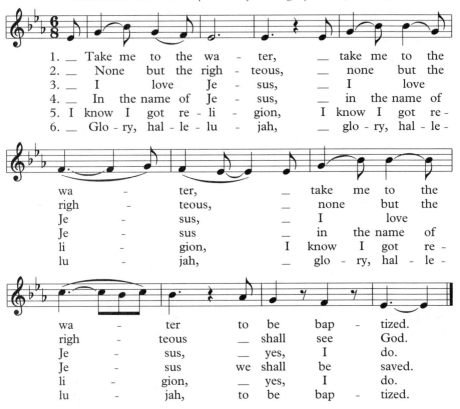

1. __ Take me to the wa - ter, __ take me to the
2. __ None but the righ - teous, __ none but the
3. __ I love Je - sus, __ I love
4. __ In the name of Je - sus, __ in the name of
5. I know I got re - li - gion, I know I got re -
6. __ Glo - ry, hal - le - lu - jah, __ glo - ry, hal - le -

wa - ter, __ take me to the
righ - teous, __ none but the
Je - sus, __ I love
Je - sus __ in the name of
li - gion, I know I got re -
lu - jah, __ glo - ry, hal - le -

wa - ter to be bap - tized.
righ - teous __ shall see God.
Je - sus, __ yes, I do.
Je - sus we shall be saved.
li - gion, __ yes, I do.
lu - jah, to be bap - tized.

WORDS: African American traditional   TO THE WATER
MUSIC: African American traditional, arr. by Marilyn E. Thornton   Irregular
Arr. © 2007 Abingdon Press, admin. by The Copyright Co.

191 Wash, O God, Our Sons and Daughters

But when they believed Philip, who was proclaiming the good news about the kingdom of God
and the name of Jesus Christ, they were baptized, both men and women. (Acts 8:12)

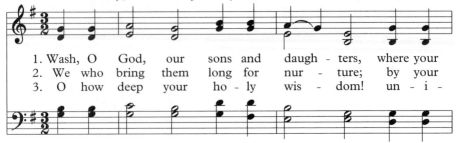

1. Wash, O God, our sons and daugh - ters, where your
2. We who bring them long for nur - ture; by your
3. O how deep your ho - ly wis - dom! un - i -

WORDS: Ruth Duck   BEACH SPRING
MUSIC: Attr. to B. F. White, harm. by Ronald A. Nelson   8 7 8 7
Words © 1989 The United Methodist Publishing House; harm. © 1978 *Lutheran Book of Worship*

cleans - ing wa - ters flow. Num-ber them a - mong your
milk may we be fed. Let us join your feast, par -
mag - gined, all your ways! To your name be glo - ry,

peo - ple; bless as Christ blessed long a - go. Weave them
tak - ing cup of bless - ing, liv - ing bread. God, re -
hon - or! With our lives we wor-ship praise! We your

gar - ments bright and spar - kling; Com - pass
new us, guide our foot - steps; free from
peo - ple stand be - fore you, wa - ter -

them with love and light. Fill a - noint them; send your
sin and all its snares, one with Christ in liv - ing,
washed and Spir - it - born. By your grace, our lives we

Spir - it, Ho - ly dove and heart's de - light.
dy - ing, by your Spir - it, chil - dren, heirs.
of - fer. Re - cre - ate us; God, trans - form!

192   I've Just Come from the Fountain

"To the thirsty I will give water as a gift from the spring of the water of life." (Revelation 21:6*b*)

2. O sister, do you love Jesus ...
3. O sinner, do you love Jesus ...

WORDS: African American spiritual
MUSIC: African American spiritual, arr. by James Capers
Arr. © 1995 Augsburg Fortress

HIS NAME SO SWEET
88.74 with Refrain

Je - sus? His name's so sweet. O Lord, I've

Water Flowing Free 193

Then the angel showed me the river of the water of life, bright as crystal,
flowing from the throne of God and of the Lamb. (Revelation 22:1)

1. Wa-ter flow - ing, flow - ing free, streams of
2. Like the flood up - on the earth claim-ing
3. Not like Na - maan or like John; graced by
4. Wa-ter flow - ing, flow - ing free, streams of

wa - ter flows for me. cleans - ing wa - ter, free - ing strife,
life and giv - ing birth; quench-ing thirst - y souls with - in,
God's own bless - ed Son. Wa - ter from his bleed - ing side;
wa - ter flows for me. Washed for - ev - er by his blood;

liv - ing wa - ter, sav - ing life. God's a - maz - ing
free - ing hearts from guilt and sin. Full re - demp - tion
Je - sus' love for all a - bides. Born in Christ a -
bathed for - ev - er in his love. Blessed with spir - it

grace, poured for A - dam's race.
free, bought for you and me.
new life for me and you.
power, life for - ev - er - more.

WORDS: Gennifer Benjamin Brooks
MUSIC: Mark A. Miller

WATER BROOKS
77.77 55

194 Certainly, Lord

WORDS: African American spiritual
MUSIC: African American spiritual, arr. by Cynthia Wilson
Arr. © 2007 Abingdon Press, admin. by The Copyright Co.

CERTAINLY LORD
7 4 7 4 7 4 10

We Welcome You

"Whoever welcomes you welcomes me,
and whoever welcomes me welcomes the one who sent me." (Matthew 10:40)

1. We wel - come you to the ta - ble of our
2. We love you with the love of Je - sus

Lord. We wel-come you to the Feast of Thanks-giv -
Christ. We love you by the power of the Spir -

ing. Oh, the cup of sal - va - tion, the
it. Oh, the Fa - ther, the Son, the

bread that comes from heaven. We wel - come
Ho - ly Spir - it's one. We love

you to the ta - ble of God. ____
you with the love of God. ____

WORDS: Marilyn E. Thornton
MUSIC: Marilyn E. Thornton

196   Jesus Is Here Right Now

"For where two or three are gathered in my name, I am there among them." (Matthew 18:20)

WORDS: Leon Roberts
MUSIC: Leon Roberts

Glory to His Name

197

It is sown in dishonor, it is raised in glory. (1 Corinthians 15:43a)

WORDS: Elisha Hoffman
MUSIC: John H. Stockton, arr. by Monya Davis Logan
Arr. © 2007 Abingdon Press, admin. by The Copyright Co.

GLORY TO HIS NAME
999 7 with Refrain

198 Halleluya! Pelo Tsa Rona

For this I will extol you, O LORD, among the nations,
and sing praises to your name. (2 Samuel 22:50)

Refrain

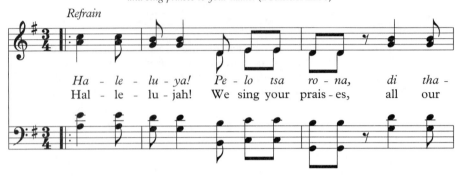

Ha - le - lu - ya!   Pe - lo   tsa   ro - na,   di   tha -
Hal - le - lu - jah!   We sing your prais - es,   all   our

bi - le   ka - o - fe - la.   Ha - le - lu - ya!   Pe - lo   tsa
hearts are filled with glad - ness.   Hal - le - lu - jah!   We sing your

ro - na,   di   tha - bi - le   ka - o - fe - la.
prais - es,   all   our hearts are filled with glad - ness.

African Phonetics
Refrain
Hah-lay-loo-yah! Pay-loh tsah roh-nah, de tah-bil-lay kah-oh-fay-lay. *(twice)*

Verses
1. Lay Mow-ray-nay Jay-zoh, yah ray doo-may-layt-sang,
   yah ray doo-may-layt-sang, hoh tsah-mah-sah ay-vahn-heh-dee.
2. Oh nah nah lay boh mahng? Lay bah-roo-too-wah bah hah-ay. *(twice)*

Verses

1. Ke Mo - re - na Je - so, ya re
2. O na na le bo mang? Le ba -
1. Christ the Lord to us said: I am
2. Now he sends us all out, strong in

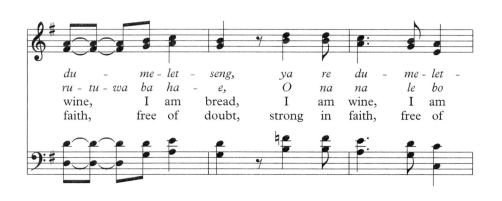

du - me - let - seng, ya re du - me - let -
ru - tu - wa ba ha - e, O na na le bo
wine, I am bread, I am wine, I am
faith, free of doubt, strong in faith, free of

seng ho tsa - mai - sa e - van - ge di.
mang? Le ba - ru - tu - wa ba ha - e.
bread, give to all who thirst and hun - ger.
doubt, to pro - claim the joy - ful Gos - pel.

199 Broken for Me

And when he had given thanks, he broke it and said,
"This is my body that is for you." (1 Corinthians 11:24a)

Bro-ken for me, _____ bro-ken for

Last time to Coda ⊕

you, the bod-y of Je - sus, _____

— bro-ken for you.

1. He of-fered his
2. _ Come to my
3. _ This is my
4. _ This is my

bod - y; _____ he poured out his soul;
ta - ble _____ _ and with me dine;
bod - y _____ _ giv - en for you;
blood _____ _ I shed for you,

D.C.

Je - sus was bro - ken _____ that we might be whole.
eat of my bread _____ and drink of my wine.
eat it re-mem - bering _ I died for you.
for your for-give - ness, ___ mak-ing you new.

⊕ CODA

the bod-y of Je - sus, _____ bro-ken for you.

WORDS: Janet Lunt
MUSIC: Janet Lunt
© 1978 Sovereign Music UK

BROKEN FOR ME
Irregular with Refrain

A Perfect Sacrifice

He has appeared once for all at the end of the age
to remove sin by the sacrifice of himself. (Hebrews 9:26*b*)

1. Ho - ly One, _ Je - sus Christ, _____ the on - ly One _

2. Lord I yield, _ yes, I give _ this my song, _

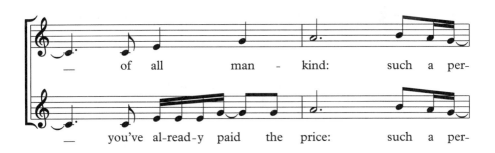

_ wor-thy to give his life, _____ for the sins _

_____ my praise of sac - ri - fice. _ I give you my life, _

_ of all man - kind: such a per-

_ you've al-read-y paid the price: such a per-

fect sac - ri - fice, Je - sus Christ! _

fect sac - ri - fice, Je - sus Christ! _

WORDS: Michael McKay
MUSIC: Michael McKay, arr. by Nolan Williams, Jr.

201   I Know It Was the Blood

In him we have redemption through his blood, the forgiveness of our trespasses,
according to the riches of his grace. (Ephesians 1:7)

WORDS: Trad. African American
MUSIC: Trad. African American, arr. by Marilyn E. Thornton
Arr. © 2007 Abingdon Press, admin. by The Copyright Co.

IT WAS THE BLOOD
66 8 with Refrain

Grace Flows Down

202

From his fullness we have all received, grace upon grace. (John 1:16)

A - maz - ing grace, _____ how sweet the sound; _

_ a - maz - ing love, _____

now flow - ing down _ from hands and feet _ that were

nailed to the tree _____ as grace flows down _

and cov - ers me. _ It cov - ers me, _____

_____ it cov - ers me, _____

_____ it cov - ers me, _____

_____ it cov - ers me.

WORDS: David Bell, Louis Giglio, and Rod Padgett
MUSIC: David Bell, Louie Giglio, and Rod Padgett

203 In Remembrance

"This cup is the new covenant in my blood.
Do this, as often as you drink it, in remembrance of me." (1 Corinthians 11:25b)

1. In re - mem-brance of me, eat this bread. _____ In re -
2. In re -) mem-brance of me, heal the sick. _____ In re -

mem-brance of me, drink this wine. _____ In re -
mem-brance of me, feed the poor. _____ In re -

mem-brance of me, pray for the time when
mem-brance of me, o - pen the door and

God's own will is done. _____ 2. In re -
let your broth - er

WORDS: Ragan Courtney
MUSIC: Buryl Red

RED
Irregular

© 1972 Broadman Press, assigned to Van Ness Press, Inc. (admin. by LifeWay Worship Music Group)

The Blood Will Never Lose Its Power 204

To him who loves us and freed us from our sins by his blood. (Revelation 1:5*b*)

1. The blood that Je - sus shed for me,
(2. It) soothes my doubts and calms my fears,

way back on Cal - va - ry, }
and it dries all my tears, }
the blood that gives me

strength from day to day, it will nev - er

Refrain

lose its power. ___ It reach - es to the high - est

moun-tain, ___ it flows to the low - est val - ley; ___

___ the blood that gives me strength from day to

day, it will nev - er lose its power. 2. It

power. Oh, it will nev - er lose its power. ___

WORDS: Andraé Crouch
MUSIC: Andraé Crouch

THE BLOOD
86 10 7 with Refrain

205 Taste and See

O taste and see that the LORD is good;
happy are those who take refuge in him. (Psalm 34:8)

WORDS: James E. Moore, Jr.
MUSIC: James E. Moore, Jr.

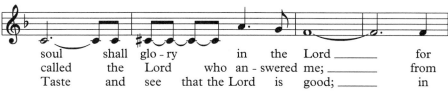

soul   shall   glo - ry   in   the   Lord _____   for
called   the   Lord   who an - swered me; _____ from
Taste   and   see that the Lord is   good; _____   in

D.C.

God   has   been   so good to   me. _____
all   my trou-bles I was set   free. _____
God   we   need put all our   trust. _____

Let Us Talents and Tongues Employ   206

And all of them ate and were filled;
and they took up the broken pieces left over, seven baskets full. (Matthew 15:37)

1. Let us tal - ents and tongues em - ploy. Reach-ing out with a
2. Christ is a - ble to   make us one.   At the ta - ble he
3. Je - sus calls us in, sends us out   bear - ing fruit in a

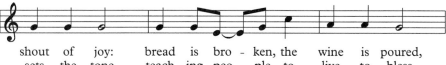

shout   of   joy: bread is bro - ken, the wine is poured,
sets   the tone,   teach - ing peo - ple to live to bless,
world of doubt,   gives us love to tell, bread to share:

Christ is spo - ken and seen and heard.
love   in word and in   deed ex - press. Je - sus lives a-gain,
God (Im-man - u - el)   ev - ery-where!

earth can breathe a-gain, pass the word a-round: loaves a - bound!

WORDS: Fred Kaan
MUSIC: Jamaican folk melody, adapt. by Doreen Potter
© 1975 Hope Publishing Co.

LINSTEAD
LM with Refrain

207-a   Communion Setting

"Hosanna to the Son of David! Blessed is the one
who comes in the name of the Lord! Hosanna in highest heaven! (Matthew 21:9b)

(Preface)

Leader ... *All*

The Lord be with you. ___ And al - so with you. ___ Lift up your hearts. ___ We lift them up to the Lord. ___ Let us give thanks to the Lord our God. It is right to give our thanks and praise. _____

WORDS: From *The United Methodist Hymnal*
MUSIC: Mark A. Miller

Music © 2000 Abingdon Press, admin. by The Copyright Co.

207-b   (Sanctus)

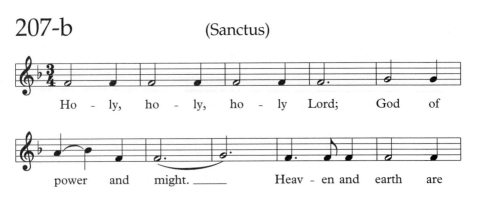

Ho - ly, ho - ly, ho - ly Lord; God of power and might. ___ Heav - en and earth are

WORDS: From *The United Methodist Hymnal* (Isa. 6:3; Matt. 21:9)
MUSIC: Mark A. Miller

Music © 1999 Abingdon Press, admin. by The Copyright Co.

full of your glo - ry. _____ Ho -
san - na in the high - est! Ho - san - na in the high - est! Ho -
san - na in the high - est! _____ Blest is the
one who comes _____ in the name of the
Lord. _____ Ho - san - na in the high - est! Ho - san - na in the
high - est! Ho - san - na in the high - est! _____

(Memorial Acclamation) 207-c

Christ has died, Christ is ris - en, Christ will
come a - gain. _____ Ho - san - na in the high - est! Ho -
san - na in the high-est! Ho - san - na in the high - est! _____

WORDS: From *The United Methodist Hymnal*
MUSIC: Mark A. Miller

207-d   (Great Amen)

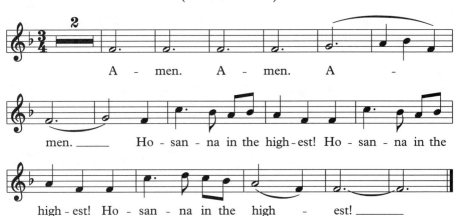

A - men.   A - men.   A -

men. _____   Ho - san - na in the high - est! Ho - san - na in the

high - est! Ho - san - na in the high - est! _____

WORDS: From *The United Methodist Hymnal*
MUSIC: Mark A. Miller

Music © 1999 Abingdon Press, admin. by The Copyright Co.

208   O, How He Loves You and Me

*"For God so loved the world that he gave his only Son,
so that everyone who believes in him may not perish but may have eternal life.* (John 3:16)

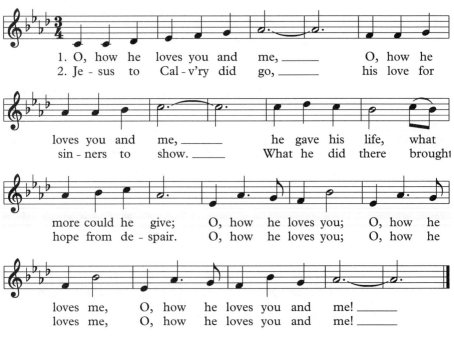

1. O, how he loves you and me, _____ O, how he
2. Je - sus to Cal - v'ry did go, _____ his love for

loves you and me, _____ he gave his life, what
sin - ners to show. _____ What he did there brought

more could he give; O, how he loves you; O, how he
hope from de - spair. O, how he loves you; O, how he

loves me, O, how he loves you and me! _____
loves me, O, how he loves you and me! _____

WORDS: Kurt Kaiser
MUSIC: Kurt Kaiser, arr. by William S. Moon

© 1975 Word Music, LLC

PATRICIA
Irregular

Psalm 19:14

Let the words of my mouth and the meditation of my heart be acceptable to you,
O LORD, my rock and my redeemer. (Psalm 19:14)

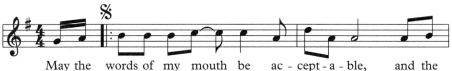

May the words of my mouth be ac - cept - a - ble, and the

med - i - ta-tions of my heart _ be ac - cept-a-ble, be ac -

cept - a - ble, ac - cept - a - ble, Lord, to

|1| |2| *to next section* | *Last time* | *Fine* |

you. May the you. you.

Oh, my Lord, _ to your Spir - it I sur - ren -

der. May the ser - vice that I ren - der be ac -

|1| |2| *D.S. al Fine*

cept-a-ble, Lord, to you. you. May the

WORDS: Regina Hoosier
MUSIC: Regina Hoosier

210 Acceptable to You

Let the words of my mouth and the meditations of my heart be acceptable to you,
O LORD, my rock and my redeemer. (Psalm 19:14)

WORDS: Eli Wilson, Jr.
MUSIC: Eli Wilson, Jr., arr. by Darryl Glenn Nettles

© 1989 Eli Wilson Ministries

and my words, Lord, __ ac-cept-a - ble to thee.

What Shall I Render? 211

What shall I return to the LORD for all his bounty to me? (Psalm 116:12)

1. What shall I ren - der un - to
2. All I can ren - der is my

God for all his mer-cies? __ What shall I
bod - y and my soul. That's all I can

ren - der, tell me what shall I give?
ren - der, that's all I can give.

God has ev-ery-thing; ev-ery-thing be-longs to him.

What shall I ren-der, tell me what shall I give?

WORDS: Margaret Pleasant Douroux
MUSIC: Margaret Pleasant Douroux

© 1975 Margaret Pleasant Douroux

212 Offering

Present your bodies as a living sacrifice,
holy and acceptable to God, which is your spiritual worship. (Romans 12:1b)

Repeat as desired

To continue

If you're of - fer - ing just an - y - thing then you're giv - ing some - thing less. You should of - fer God your ev - ery - thing, of - fer - ing to him your best. The best of your o - be - di - ence, the best of your time, the best of your heart with love. The best of your o - be - di - ence, the best of your time, the

WORDS: Toby Hill
MUSIC: Toby Hill
© 2005 Toby Hill

213   We Bring the Sacrifice of Praise

Through Jesus, therefore, let us continually offer to God a sacrifice of praise—
the fruit of lips that confess his name. (Hebrews 13:15 NIV)

We bring the sac-ri-fice of praise in-to the house of the Lord.

We bring the sac-ri-fice of praise in-to the house of the Lord. And we

of - fer up to you the sac-ri - fic - es of thanks-giv-ing, and we

of - fer up to you the sac-ri - fic - es of praise.

WORDS: Kirk Dearman
MUSIC: Kirk Dearman, arr. by Stephen Key

Praise God, from Whom All Blessings Flow 214

Praise the LORD! How good it is to sing praises to our God;
for he is gracious, and a song of praise is fitting. (Psalm 147:1)

Praise God, from whom all bless - ings flow;

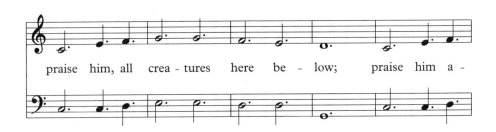

praise him, all crea - tures here be - low; praise him a -

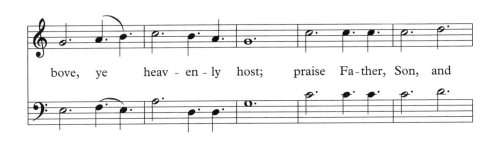

bove, ye heav - en - ly host; praise Fa - ther, Son, and

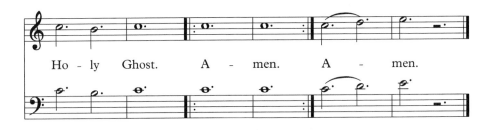

Ho - ly Ghost. A - men. A - men.

WORDS: Thomas Ken, adapt. from Isaac Watts and William Kethe
MUSIC: Adapt. from John Hatton by George Coles, arr. by Monya Davis Logan
© 1968 Roberta Martin

215   God Be with You

May the grace of our Lord Jesus Christ be with your spirit,
brothers and sisters. Amen. (Galatians 6:18)

WORDS: Thomas A. Dorsey
MUSIC: Thomas A. Dorsey, arr. by Horace Clarence Boyer

© 1940 (renewed) Warner-Tamerlane Publishing Corp.; arr. © 2006 Warner-Tamerlane Publishing Corp.

If You Say Go

216

Now by this we may be sure that we know him, if we obey his commandments. (1 John 2:3)

WORDS: Diane Thiel
MUSIC: Diane Thiel, arr. by William S. Moon

217 Prepare Us, Lord

So we are ambassadors for Christ,
since God is making his appeal through us. (2 Corinthians 5:20a)

Pre - pare us, Lord, ___ to be your in - stru-ment; ___

___ Pre - pare us, Lord, ___ to be like you.

Pre - pare us, Lord, ___ that we might tru - ly re - pre -

sent the church of Je - sus Christ ___ to the world.

For a - bun - dant life ___ and de -

liv - er - ance ___ for your peo - ple

WORDS: Eli Wilson, Jr.
MUSIC: Eli Wilson, Jr.
© 1990 Eli Wilson, Jr.

will come as we pre-pare our - selves in you. _____

As You Go, Tell the World 218

As you go, proclaim the good news, "The kingdom of heaven has come near." (Matthew 10:7)

Unison   *Fine*

As you go, _ telll the world, _ as you go, _ tell the world. _

Parts

Tell the world a-bout Je - sus, tell them a - bout his love.

D.C.

Tell the world a-bout Je - sus, tell them a - bout his love.

WORDS: Anonymous
MUSIC: Anonymous, arr. by Valeria A. Foster

219   I Need You to Survive

Above all, clothe yourselves with love . . . . And let the peace of Christ rule in your hearts,
to which indeed you were called in the one body. (Colossians 3:14-15a)

I need you, you need me,

we're all a part of God's bod - y,

stand with me, a - gree with me,

we're all a part of God's bod - y.

It is God's will that ev - ery need _

_____ be sup-plied, you are im - por -

tant to me, I need you to sur - vive, _

WORDS: David Frazier
MUSIC: David Frazier, arr. by Mark A. Miller
© God's Music, Inc.

Honor and Glory

To the King of the ages, immortal, invisible, the only God,
be honor and glory forever and ever. Amen. (1 Timothy 1:17)

WORDS: Gary Oliver
MUSIC: Gary Oliver

vis - i - ble, the on - ly God, be the

hon - or and glo - ry for - ev - er and

Chorus

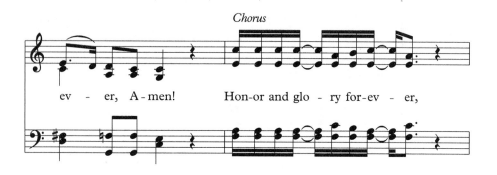

ev - er, A - men! Hon-or and glo - ry for-ev - er,

hon - or and glo - ry for - ev - er;

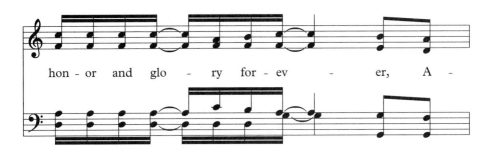

hon - or and glo - ry for - ev - er, A -

men! Hon-or and glo - ry for - ev - er,

hon - or and glo - ry for - ev - er;

hon-or and glo - ry for-ev - er, A - men!

221 Alpha and Omega

"I am the Alpha and the Omega, the first and the last, the beginning and the end." (Revelation 22:13)

WORDS: Erasmus Mutanbira
MUSIC: Trad. African, transcribed by William S. Moon

© 2005 Sound of the New Breed, admin. by Integrity's Praise! Music (BMI)

Acknowledgments

Use of copyrighted material is gratefully acknowledged by the publisher. Every effort has been made to locate the administrator of each copyright. The publisher would be pleased to have any errors or omissions brought to its attention. All copyright notices include the following declarations. All rights reserved. International copyright secured. Used with permission.

Abingdon Press (see The Copyright Company)
Doris Akers (see Unichappell Music)
Albert E. Brumley & Sons (see ICG)
Alfred Publishing, P.O. Box 10003, Van Nuys, CA 91410-0003
Amity Music
Ariose Music (see EMI CMG Publishing)
Augsburg Fortress Publishers, P.O. Box 1209, Minneapolis, MN 55440-1209; (612) 330-3300
B4 Entertainment, Rich Burchell, P.O. Box 331423, Murfreesboro, TN 37133; (615) 217-4711; rickyb@b4entertainment.com
BMG (ASCAP) (see Music Services)
BMG Songs, Inc. (see Music Services)
Birdwing Music (see EMI CMG Publishing)
Bob Jay Publishing, c/o Rodney L. Adams, P.O. Box 515, Lincolnton Station, New York, NY 10037-0514; (212) 283-4980; Bobjay7412@aol.com
Boosey & Co. (see Boosey & Hawkes, Inc.)
Boosey & Hawkes, Inc., 35 East 21st St., New York, NY 10010; (212) 358-5300
Brentwood-Benson Music Publishing, Inc. (see Music Services)
Bridge Building Music (see Brentwood-Benson Music Publishing)
Broadman Press (see Van Ness Press)
Gennifer Benjamin Brooks, Garrett Evangelical Theology Seminary, 2121 Sheridan Rd., Evanston, IL 60201
Bud John Songs (see EMI CMG Publishing)
Bud John Tunes, Inc. (see EMI CMG Publishing)
CMI-HP Publishing (see Word Music, LLC)
Caribbean Conference of Churches, P.O. Box 867, Port of Spain, Trinidad; (866) 623-0588; trinidad-headoffice@ccc-caribe.org
Carlin America, 126 East 38th St., New York, NY 10016
Carol Joy Music (see ICG)

Century Oak Publishing Group (see MCS America)
Changing Church Forum, 13901 Fairview Dr., Burnsville, MN 55337; (800) 874-2044, FAX (612) 435-8015; changing@changingchurch.org
Michael L. Charles, 5717 NE Quartz Dr., Lees Summit, MO 64064
Chinwah Songs (see Executive Publishing Administration)
Cecilia L. Clemons; c/o Tracyton United Methodist Church; P.O. Box 127; Tracyton, WA 98393
J. Jefferson Cleveland, Estate of J. Jefferson Cleveland, c/o William B. McCain, 4500 Massachusetts Ave. NW, Washington, DC 20016
Colette Coward, 336 Meadow Glen Drive, Bear, DE 19701
Crouch Music (see EMI CMG Publishing)
Pamela Jean Davis, 1502 Fountain Lake Dr., #627, Stafford, TX 77477
Dayspring Music, LLC (see Word Music, LLC)
Dixon Music, Rev. Jessy Dixon, 3240 Danne Rd., Crete, IL 60417; (708) 672-8682
Donn Charles Thomas Publishing, Messiah's World Outreach Ministries, P.O. Box 594, Stone Mountain, GA 30086; (404) 299-8005; dthomas801@aol.com
Doulos Publishing (see Maranatha! Music)
Dr. Margaret Pleasant Douroux, Rev. Earl Pleasant Publishing, P.O. Box 3247, Thousand Oaks, CA 91359; (818) 991-3728, FAX (818) 991-2567
Jonathan Cole Dow, c/o Aldersgate Renewal Ministries, 121 East Ave., Goodlettsville, TN 37072
EMI CMG, P.O. Box 5085, Brentwood, TN 37024-5085
Edward B. Marks Music Co. (see Carlin America)
Executive Publishing Administration, 10220 Glade Ave., Chatsworth, CA 91311
Full Armor Music (see The Kruger Organization)
Gaither Copyright Management, P.O. Box 737, Alexandria, IN 46001; (765) 724-8233, FAX (765) 724-8290

Gamut Music Productions, 704 Saddle Trail Ct., Hermitage, TN 37076
General Board of Global Ministries (see Hope Publishing)
GIA Publications, Inc., 7404 S. Mason Ave., Chicago, IL 60638; (708) 496-3800
God's Music, c/o Li'l Dave's Music, 6 Gramaton Ave., 5th Floor, Mount Vernon, NY 10550
Grace Fellowship (see Maranatha! Music)
Hal Leonard, P.O. Box 13819, Milwaukee, WI 53213
Harvest Fire Music (see Integrity's Praise! Music)
Toby Hill, 7410 Oak Walk Dr., Humble, TX 77346
Hillsongs Publishing (see Integrity Music)
Hope Publishing Company, 380 S. Main Pl., Carol Stream, IL 60188; (800) 323-1049, FAX (630) 665-2552; www.hopepublishing.com
Regina Hoosier, P.O. Box 30094, Clarksville TN 37040; yielded@bellsouth.net
House Of Mercy Music (see Music Services)
J. Edward Hoy ICG, P.O. Box 24149, Nashville, TN 37202
Integrity Music, Inc., 1000 Cody Rd., Mobile, AL 36695-3425; (334) 633-9000, FAX (334) 633-9998
Intergrity's Hosanna! Music (see Integrity Music, Inc.)
Intergrity's Praise! Music (see Integrity Music, Inc.)
International Atlanta Music (see Malaco Music)
JDI Music (see JRobersongs Music)
Jeff Ferguson Music (see ICG)
John T. Benson Publishing Co. (see Music Services)
Jonathan Mark Music (see Gaither Copyright Management)
JRobersongs Music, P.O. Box 48105, Los Angeles, CA 90048
K Cartunes Music (see Lilly Mack Music)
Kevin Mayhew Ltd., Buxhall, Stowmarket, Suffolk, UK IP14 3DJ
Kingsman's Thankyou Music (see EMI CMG Publishing)
Latter Rain Music (see EMI CMG Publishing)

ACKNOWLEDGMENTS

Lehsem Songs (see ICG)

Leon Lewis, 10500 Fountain Lake Dr., Stafford, TX 77477

Life Song Music Press (see Music Services)

Life Spring Music, 907 McCall St., Conroe, TX 77301

Lifeway Christian Resources, One Lifeway Plaza MSN160, Nashville, TN 37234

Lilly Mack Music (BMI), 421 E. Beach, Inglewood, CA 90302; (310) 677-5603, FAX (310) 677-0250

Monya Davis Logan, 3810 York St., Dallas, TX 75210-2736

Ludlow Music, Inc., c/o The Richmond Organization, 266 West 37th Street, 17th Floor, New York, NY 10018-6609

MCS America, 1625 Broadway, 4th Floor, Nashville, TN 37203; janice.bain@mcsamerica.net

MWP Publishing (see JRobersongs Music)

Malaco Music, P.O. Box 9287, Jackson, MS 39286-9281; (601) 982-4522, FAX (601) 982-4528

Manna Music, 35255 Brooten Rd., Pacific City, OR 97135; (503) 965-6112

Maranatha! Music (see Music Services)

Maranatha! Praise, Inc. (see Music Services)

Martha Munizzi Music (see Say The Name Publishing)

Roberta Martin (see Unichappell Music)

Martin and Morris Studio, Inc. (see Unichappell Music)

Patrick Matsikenyiri, No. 13 Cripps Rd., Palmertón, Mutare, Zimbabwe; (540) 514-6359

Meadowgreen Music (see EMI CMG Publishing)

Meaux Mercy (see EMI CMG Publishing)

Mercy/Vineyard Music (see Music Services)

Mark A. Miller, 1118 Gresham Rd., Plainfield, NJ 07062

Mo' Berrie Publishing, P.O. Box 818, Summit, MS 39666 (601) 684-0117

William S. Moon, 909 Halcyon Avenue, Nashville, TN 37204

Mountain Spring Music (see EMI CMG Publishing)

Music Services, Inc. (ASCAP), 1526 Otter Creek Rd., Nashville, TN 37215

New Song Music, P.O. Box 116, Lawai, HI 96765

New Spring Publishing (see Brentwood-Benson Music Publishing)

Verolga Nix, 931 E. Sedgwick St., Philadelphia, PA 19150-3517; (215) 248-2728

Nory B Publishing (see Malaco Music)

Johnetta Johnson Page, 4927 Silen Lake Dr., San Antonio, TX 78244

Paragon Music (seee Brentwood-Benson Music Publishing)

Raise Publishing Co., Raymond Wise, 197 Monarch Dr., Pataskala, OH 43062

Richwood Music (see MCS America)

Ron Harris Music, c/o Ron Harris, 22643 Paul Revere Dr., Calabasas, CA 91302

Sanabella Music (see EMI CMG Publishing)

Say The Name Publishing, c/o Nick Kroger, 575 Dunmar Circle, Winter Springs, FL 32708-3905; (407) 834-5620, FAX (407) 673-5620; saythename@hotmail.com

Schaff Music Publishing, 14 Sullivans Lane, Missouri City, TX 77459

Scripture In Song (see Maranatha! Music)

Shepherd's Heart Music (see Dayspring Music, LLC)

sixsteps music (see EMI CMG Publishing)

Sound III (see Universal Music)

Sound of Gospel

Sound of the New Breed (see Integrity's Praise! Music)

Sovereign Grace Praise (see Integrity's Praise! Music)

Sovereign Music UK, P.O. Box 356, Leighton Buzzard, BEDS, LU7 8WP, UK; sovereignm@aol.com

Spoone Music (see Word Music, LLC)

Stamps-Baxter Music (see Brentwood-Benson Music Publishing)

Straightway Music (see EMI CMG Publishing)

T. Autumn Music (see Zomba Songs)

TMMI (see Music Services)

Tedd T BMI Publishing Designedd (see EMI CMG Publishing)

The Church of God in Christ Publishing Board

The Copyright Company, 1025 16th Ave. South, Suite 204, Nashville, TN 37212; FAX (615) 244-5591; lynda.pearson@thecopyrightco.com

The Iona Community (Scotland) (see GIA Publications, Inc.)

The Kruger Organization, Inc., 15 Rolling Way, New City, NY 10956-6912; (202) 966-3280, FAX (202) 364-1367; publishing@tkgoup.com

Marilyn E. Thornton, The United Methodist Publishing House, 201 8th Ave. South, Nashville, TN 37202

Cecilia Olusola Tribble, c/o Marilyn E. Thornton, The United Methodist Publishing House, 201 8th Ave. South, Nashville, TN 37202

Unichappell Music (see Alfred Publishing)

Universal MCA Music Publishing (see Universal Music)

Universal Music Publishing (see Hal Leonard)

Utryck (see Walton Music Group)

Van Ness Press (see Lifeway Christian Resources)

Vineyard Songs (see Music Services)

WGRG The Iona Community (Scotland) (see GIA Publications, Inc.)

Walton Music Group, 1028 Highland Woods Rd., Chapel Hill, NC 27517; (919) 929-1330

Wayne Leupold Editions, 8510 Triad Dr., Colfax, NC 27235

Warner-Tamerlane Publishing (see Alfred Publishing)

We Lyke Music, 3001 West 82nd Pl., Inglewood, CA 90305

Wendell Whalum, The Estate of Wendell Whalum, c/o Clarie Whalum, 2439 Greenwood Circle, East Point, GA 30344

Whole Armor Music (see The Kruger Organization)

Willow Branch Publishing (see Gaither Copyright Management)

Brian C. Wilson, 1811 Villa Del Lago, Missouri City, TX 77459

Cynthia Wilson, 2786 Keystone Ave., Lithonia, GA 30058

Eli Wilson, Jr., Eli Wilson Ministries, P.O. Box 680172, Orlando, FL 32868-0712

Word Music, LLC, 20 Music Square East, Nashville, TN 37203; (615) 733-1880, FAX (615) 733-1885; luann.inman@warnerchappell.com worshiptogether.com songs (see EMI CMG Publishing)

Wythrne Music (see JRobersongs Music)

Y'Shua Publishing

Darlene Zschech (see Integrity Music)

Topical Index

224

TOPICAL INDEX

Index of First Lines and Common Titles

ISBN-13: 978-0-687-33527-5